K-P⏾ETRY
Getting on the Wings of Peace
한국시 평화의 날개 달다

2024
한국문인협회
문학정보화위원회

Congratulatory Address

A Poem Can Make the World Brighter and More Fragrant

Novelist & President of The Korean Writers Association
Kim Ho-woon

It's already summer in all green before we get quite ready to let go of beautiful and floral spring with flowers in full bloom. But beyond the changing season, our literature is always here, breathing in the heart of people.

I have heard a good news that the literary informatization committee of The Korean Writers Association has published an anthology of K-Poetry with the title, "Korean Poetry Getting on the Wings of Peace," which will introduce great Korean poems translated into English to foreign readers. I like to express my respectful thanks to the committee chairperson Jee Eun-kyung and all the people concerned with for their efforts to publish this anthology.

Nowadays, many people worry about general readers who are getting away from reading literature. According to statistics being issued every year, the percentage of reading population continues to be in decrease and so is the percentage of literature readers. The society having no reading population is like a desert. Without reading population, there would be no bridge that connects people to each other. I believe that a piece of literary work is like a tree. Without trees, our mother planet, the Earth, becomes a desert where we can't live any more. As we all know, we can't live in the desolate places like a desert.

With lesser reading population, our society would be turned into a place like a barren desert.

At the time like this, I was delightful to hear the news that Anthology of Korean Poetry Getting on the Wings of Peace has been published, and I am sure that this anthology would definitely make our society more rich and fertile like sweet rain does to the land during the drought. Especially when Korean culture is being loved by all people, beautiful poems translated and presented in this anthology will convey our cultural fragrance to the hearts of foreign readers.

As of now, we are witnessing ongoing wars at the conflicting areas of the world, which is one of the unfortunate consequences that we have lost our compassion that connects people to each other with warm hearts. Our literature created with the loving hearts of humanity and nature can be helpful to make the chaos we are experiencing disappear from the world for good. I believe our literature has a certain role to play for that purpose. As vaccines have played great roles for us to fight against COVID 19, each and every piece of poem and our literature in general, I hope, can do the same, contributing to make our world more secure place while establish the world peace.

Again I congratulate the publication of Anthology of Korean Poetry Getting on the Wings of Peace and once again appreciate Jee Eun-kyung, chairperson of the committee and all the people concerned with the publication for their sincere efforts. Again, I really like to see that this anthology can give lights to people around the world with the messages for the world peace.

축사

한 편의 시가 세상을 밝고 향기롭게 만듭니다

소설가·한국문인협회 이사장
김 호 운

　아름답고 향기로운 꽃이 피는 봄인가 했는데 어느새 녹음綠陰이 짙은 여름이 되었습니다. 이렇듯 우리 문학은 변하는 계절과 흐르는 시간을 넘어서 그렇게 사람들의 가슴에 영원히 살아 숨 쉽니다.

　《한국문인협회 문학정보화위원회》에서 우리의 우수한 시를 번역한 k-poetry 사화집 『한국시 평화의 날개 달다』를 출간한다는 매우 기쁜 소식을 들었습니다. 어려운 시기에 훌륭한 기획으로 한국 문학을 빛내주신 지은경 위원장님을 비롯한 관계자 여러분께 존경의 마음을 담아 축하의 박수를 보냅니다.

　사람들이 책을 잘 읽지 않는다고 걱정합니다. 맞습니다. 해마다 나오는 통계에 의하면 독서 인구가 매년 줄어들고 있습니다. 독서 인구가 줄어드는 것에 비례하여 문학 작품을 읽는 독자들 수도 많이 줄어들었습니다. 책을 읽지 않는 사회는 마치 나무가 없는 사막과 같습니다. 사람과 사람을 잇는 인정의 다리가 사라져 삭막한 사회가 됩니다. 문학 작품 한 편은 나무 한 그루와 같습니다. 나무가 없으면 우리가 사는 지구는 사막이 되고, 사막에서는 사람이 살 수가 없습니다. 문학 작품을 읽는 인구가 줄어들면 줄어들수록 우리 사회는 인정이 메말라져 마치 삭막한 사막과 같이 변합니다.

이러한 때 한국 시 번역 사화집『한국시 평화의 날개 달다』를 기획 출판하는 일은 가뭄의 단비처럼 우리 사회를 밝게 빛낼 것입니다. 한국의 문화가 세계인들에게 사랑받고 있는 이때 우리의 아름다운 시가 여기에 더 깊은 문화의 향기를 전할 것입니다.

 지금 세계는 전화戰禍가 끊이질 않습니다. 이는 사람과 사람 사이를 잇는 인정이 메말라 일어나는 불행이기도 합니다. 사람과 자연을 사랑하는 마음으로 창작한 우리 문학으로 이 혼돈을 사라지게 해야 합니다. 우리 문학이 그러한 역할을 할 것입니다. 코로나19로 세계 인류가 4년여 고통을 겪었을 때 이를 극복하는 데 백신이 큰 역할을 했습니다. 우리 문학이, 우리 시 한 편 한 편이 백신과 같은 역할을 하여 인류 평화를 이루어 주기를 희망합니다.

 다시 한번 한국 시 번역 사화집『한국시 평화의 날개 달다』출간을 축하하며, 지은경 위원장님을 비롯한 관계자 여러분께 거듭 감사의 마음을 전합니다. 이 작품집이 세계인들에게 널리 전해져서 인류 평화에 한 줄기 빛이 되기를 기원합니다.

Preface

Would you enjoy the Flavor of Hangeul, reading Korean Poetry in english?

Chairperson of Literary Informatization Cmte. of The Korean Writers Association
Jee, Eun-kyung Ph.D. in literature

You must be all familiar with Korean pop singer PSY whose "Gangnam Style" with unique dancing bewitched people all over the world 12 years ago. Since then, Korean food such as Kimchi, Gimbap, Bibimbap, Dukbokki have become popular in foreign countries, too. Beside, Korean dramas and movies all became popular enough to be called sensational, and Arirang, one of the most traditional Korean songs ever also became popular world-widely. Recently, I heard that students studying at the "Language Center" of the Oxford University in UK asked the school administration to open classes for learning Korean language, and unexpectedly high schools and universities in many countries are adopting Korean language as the first or the second foreign language.

Literary Informatization Committee of The Korean Writers Association decided to publish an anthology of K-Poetry in English with the title, "Korean Poetry Getting on The Wings of Peace," as people in the world are getting interested in Korean language. After the first publication of anthology translated in English this year, we are planing to publish another anthology in French next year, in Germany the year after next and also in Japanese and in Chinese later years to come, to make people in the world appreciate our poetry in different languages. For that purpose, we welcome any Korean poets to submit their poems to participate in this project.

Ever since the ancient time, the founding ideology of Korea has been "Benefiting every mankind". The purpose of inventing Hangeul by the Great King Sejong in 1443 was to make lay people communicate each other easily, and the decision to invent Hangeul was made on the basis of humanitarianism. We are very proud of the great achievements of our ancestors, as proved in the fact that Hangeul has been chosen as the best language for its learning efficacy in the World Language Olympics. Now, Hangeul is not just for Koreans only but for all the people who are interested in our culture. The Anthology of Korean Poetry Getting on the Wings of Peace is published to help those people around the world understand Korean culture better and more easily.

The Anthology of Korean Poetry Getting on the Wings of Peace we have published for the project is to give foreign readers a chance to enjoy the taste of Hanguel reading Korean poetry in English. Even though this publication is a small step for the future, we will do our best making more efforts every year to introduce Korean poetry to the the world. I hope that Korean poetry make people around the world feel happier in their lives with common emotions introduced here in the poems we like to share. I like to see Korean poetry to be a bride built for the world peace, and I also strongly believes that this anthology would contribute to connect all people with each other and unite them into one in harmony.

Lastly, I really thank all of the Korean poets who submitted their valuable poems for the publication of this anthology, and I also thank Kim In-young, a translation committee member of International PEN, Korea Center, who have translated the poems included here in the anthology as well as other staffs who helped editing and proofreading the poems for the publication.

책을 내며

한국시, 한글의 '말맛' 좀 보세요

(사)한국문협 문학정보화위원장
지 은 경 문학박사

　한국의 대중가수 싸이의 '강남스타일'을 아시지요. 12년 전, 전 세계를 홀린 말춤을 기억하시지요. 그 후 김치, 김밥, 비빔밥, 떡볶이 등 K-푸드가 국제적으로 인기가 많습니다. 드라마·영화는 물론 K-팝은 선풍적이고, 한민족 혼이 담긴 아리랑도 세계인들이 좋아하지요. 최근엔 영국의 옥스퍼드 대학 내 '랭귀지 센터'에서 학생들의 요청에 의해 한국어가 채택되었다고 합니다. 그뿐만 아니라 세계 여러 나라에서 한글을 제1, 제2 외국어로 선택하고 있어 한국도 놀라고 있습니다.

　(사)한국문인협회 문학정보화위원회에서는 세계인들이 한국어에 많은 관심을 갖고 있어 K-Poetry 『한국시 평화의 날개 달다』를 출간하게 되었습니다. 한국시의 독특한 '말맛'을 세계인들에게 선보이는 것입니다. 올해는 영어로 번역, 내년에는 불어, 후년에는 독어, 일어, 중국어 등등 해마다 여러 나라 언어로 번역하여 세계에 내보낼 예정입니다. 작품 모집도 한국 시인이면 누구나 참여할 수 있도록 하여 빛을 보게 하는 것이 이번 행사의 목적입니다.

　대한민국의 건국이념은 '홍익인간 정신'입니다. 인류를 널리 이롭게 한다는 휴머니즘 사상입니다. 580여 년 전 세종대왕이 창제한 한글의 목적도 만백성이 쉽게 배워 지식과 정보를 교환하도록

한 것입니다. 이러한 한글이 세계문자올림픽 대회에서 과학적이고 쉽게 배울 수 있는 가장 우수한 문자로 평가받아 금메달을 차지했습니다. 한국어는 이제 한국인만의 것이 아니게 되었습니다. 한국어에 관심 있는 분들이 『한국시 평화의 날개 달다』를 만나면 한국 문화를 좀 더 쉽게 이해할 수 있을 것입니다.

　이번에 첫 출간하는 『한국시 평화의 날개 달다』는 한글의 아름다운 '말맛'을 세계인에게 선보이는 미래의 보고서입니다. 올해 첫 출발로 미약한 부분이 있지만 매년 보완 추진 확장해 나갈 예정입니다. 한국시가 인류 보편적 가치로 세상 사람들을 위로하고 행복하게 하면 좋겠습니다. 지구는 하나, 인류도 하나, 한국시가 세계와 하나 되기를 희망합니다. 한국시가 세계를 잇는 평화의 다리 역할을 할 것을 굳게 믿습니다.

　참여해 주신 한국 시인 여러분 고맙습니다.
　번역해 주신 국제펜한국본부 번역위원 김인영 선생님의 노고에 감사드립니다.
　그 외 편집, 감수 등 도와주신 여러분의 인연에 감사드립니다.

Contents

Congratulatory Address 축사
A Poem Can Make the World Brighter and More Fragrant
한 편의 시가 세상을 밝고 향기롭게 만듭니다 Kim Ho-woon 김호운

Preface 책을 내며
Would you enjoy the Taste of Hangeul,
reading Korean Poetry in english?
한국시, 한글의 '말맛' 좀 보세요 Jee Eun-kyung 지은경

22	Sunlight 햇빛	Kang Bong-hwan 강봉환
24	A Small House of Mine 나의 작은 집	Kang Elly 강에리
26	Time 세월	Kang Yeong-deok 강영덕
28	An Icicle 고드름	Kang Chang-seok 강창석
30	A Dandelion's Territory 민들레 영토	Go Geum-seok 고금석
32	Cape Seopjikoji 섭지코지	Ko Eung-nam 고응남
34	Father's Fan Air Blower 아버지의 풍로	Ko Hwa-soon 고화순
36	Your Smile 당신의 미소	Kwak Kwang-tack 곽광택
38	The Cold Snap in Spring 꽃샘추위	Kwak Jong-chul 곽종철
40	I Like You Being a Rock 바위라서 좋다	Kwon Kyou-ho 권규호
42	A Class of Sheep 양들의 수업	Kwon Dae-ja 권대자
44	Magnolia 목련	Kim Kyung-hee 김경희
46	A Natural Burial 수목장樹木葬	Kim Kwan-sik 김관식
48	A Prologue 서시	Kim Kwan-hyung 김관형

50	Answers to Love 사랑에 대한 답 Kim Dae-eung 김대응
52	Magic Lily at Seonunsa Temple 선운사의 상사화 Kim Do-yeon 김도연
54	A Meal 밥 Kim Myung-ja 김명자
56	Dark Shades of May 오월의 그늘(시조) Kim Min-jeong 김민정
58	Waves 파도 Kim Baik-kyung 김백경
60	Yes, As of Today 그래, 오늘 Kim Bong-Kyum 김봉겸
62	Royal Azaleas Blooming in Clusters 철쭉꽃 무리 Kim Sang-cheol 김상철
64	A Dewdrop 이슬 한 방울(시조) Kim Su-yeoun 김수연
66	Song of Spring 봄 노래 Kim Ae-ran 김애란
68	The Spirits of the Olympics and Korea 올림픽 정신과 대한민국 Kim Young-soon 김영순
70	The Sounds of Rain Pouring at My Parents' Home 친정집 빗소리 Kim Young-yup 김영엽
72	March 삼월 Kim Young-weol 김영월
74	Weight of Time 시간의 무게 Kim Wang-sik 김왕식
76	Green Tea in Dream 꿈속의 차 Kim Young-kook 김용국
78	A Realization 각覺 Kim Yong-ok 김용옥
80	Porcelain Jar 항아리 Kim Woon-hyang 김운향
82	Phrases Posted to Welcome Spring 시 입춘방 Kim Yoo-jo 김유조
84	A Pond in the Sky 하늘 연못 Kim Eun-soo 김은수

Contents

86	A Space Travel 우주여행	Kim Eun-sim 김은심
88	My Father's Memory 아버지의 기억	Kim Jae-won 김재원
90	A Mirror 거울	Kim Jeong-hui 김정희
92	Let's Draw Pictures 그림 그리자(동요)	Kim Jong-hwan 김종환
94	Power of Love 사랑의 힘	Kim Jong-hee 김종희
96	Mosaic of Immersive Images 영상 모자이크	Kim Tae-ryong 김태룡
98	A Dream of New Year 새해의 꿈	Thad. T. Ghim 김태형
100	Paradise of the Elderly 노인 천국	Kim Ha-young 김하영
102	Hunger 허기	Kim Haeng-sook 김행숙
104	A Night in Spring 봄밤	Kim Hyun-sook 김현숙
106	Rose of Sarajevo 사라예보의 장미	Kim Ho-woon 김호운
108	The Sunset 저녁놀	Kim Hwan-saeng 김환생
110	Family 가족	Kim Whoo-ran 김후란
112	Time 시간	Nam Hyeon-u 남현우
114	Persimmons 홍시	Noh Sin-bae(Neung-In) 노신배
116	A Song of the Peasant's Wife 촌부의 노래	Roh Hee 노희
118	A Repairperson of the Mind 마음 수리공	Ryu In-soon 류인순
120	Persona 페르소나	Maeng Sook-young 맹숙영
122	Greeting the Sunlight 햇살 나들이	Mo Sang-cheol 모상철
124	Into the Curved Space of Time 굽은 시간 속으로	Park Kyung-hee 박경희

126	Longing 그리움 **Park Ki-im** 박기임
128	Cultivation of Relationships 인연 가꾸기 **Park Gil-dong** 박길동
130	Difference of Thought 생각의 차이 **Park Du-ik** 박두익
132	Blooming Camellia Flowers 동백 개화 **Park Mi-sum** 박미섬
134	A Lotus Flower 연꽃 **Park Byung-kyu** 박병규
136	Tears of My Mother's Life 엄마 삶의 눈물은 **Park Byeong-rae** 박병래
138	To Andromeda 안드로메다에게 **Park Seong-jin** 박성진
140	A Silkworm Cocoon 누에고치 **Park Seong-cheol** 박성철
142	The Winter of Mt. Balwangsan 발왕산의 겨울 **Park sook-ja** 박숙자
144	Love of Autumn 가을 사랑 **Park Young-kon** 박영곤
146	Love of Cosmos Flowers 코스모스 연정 **Park Won-seok** 박원석
148	Snow in Spring 춘설 **Park Eun-sun** 박은선
150	The Sound of the Coming Spring 봄이 오는 소리 **Park Jong-hwa** 박종화
152	Onions 양파 **Park jin-woo** 박진우
154	Today is Still a Great Day, Anyway 오늘이 좋아 그래도 **Park Chul-un** 박철연
156	Love Song of the Sunset 노을 연가 **Park Cheol-woo** 박철우
158	Momentary, Momentary 찰나 찰나 **Bae Sung-rok** 배성록
160	Getting Myself Lower 낮이지기 **Baek Young-ho** 백영호
162	A Lake in Tranquility 고요한 호수 **Sa Wee-hwan** 사위환

Contents

164	Tinged Bean Leaves 단풍 콩잎 Seo Yeong-hui 서영희
166	At the Riverside of The Seine in Paris 파리 세느강변에서 Sun Yu-mi 선유미
168	Arirang of Korea 대한의 아리랑 Sung Ki-hwan 성기환
170	Being in Disagreement 엇갈림 Sohn Young-ran 손영란
172	A Drinking Toast in a Loud Voice 외치는 소리 Son Jae-soo 손재수
174	In Front of Walyong Plum Tree with Dark Red Flowers 와룡매臥龍梅 검붉은 꽃잎 앞에서 Song Nak-hyun 송낙현
176	The Dream of Magnolia 목련의 꿈 Song Deok-young 송덕영
178	White Clouds 흰 구름 Song Mi-soon 송미순
180	A Flower Vase 꽃병 Song Tae-han 송태한
182	Spring Breeze 봄바람 Shin Gap-sik 신갑식
184	Grass Flowers 들꽃 Shin Young-ok 신영옥
186	Starwort Flowers 별꽃 Shin Wi-sik 신위식
188	The Sea at Splendid Dawn 새벽 바다 Sin Hye-kyung 신혜경
190	A Porcelain Jar 항아리 Ahn Kwang-suck 안광석
192	Watercolor Painting in My mind 내 마음속 수채화 Ahn Yun-ja 안윤자
194	In an Elevator 승강기 An Jae-chan 안재찬
196	A Consequence of Being Lazy 게으름의 산물 An Jong-man 안종만
198	In the Fog 안개 속에서 Ahn Hye-cho 안혜초
200	Adobe—walled Cottage 토담집 Yang Sang-gun 양상군

202	Spring Comes like an Incoming Tide 봄은 밀물처럼 온다 Yang Chang-sik 양창식
204	Feeling Tranquility 아, 고요다 Eum Chang-sup 엄창섭
206	Windflowers Blooming in Byunsan 변산 아씨 바람꽃 Yeo Woon 여 운
208	Kimchi Song 김치송 Oh Yeon-bok 오연복
210	Bibimbap 비빔밥 Woo Young-sook 우영숙
212	Dewdrops 이슬 Yoo Gyeong-ja 유경자
214	A Flower 꽃 Yoo Dong-ae 유동애
216	The Sounds of the Autumn Coming 가을이 오는 소리 Yu Sook-hee 유숙희
218	Picking Up a Life 생명을 줍다 Yu Jung-kwan 유중관
220	A Small Spring 옹달샘 Yoo Chang-geun 유창근
222	The Center of My Life 중심 Yoo Hyeong 유 형
224	Canna Seeking a Solution 칸나는 해법 모색 중 Youn Hea-jeing 윤혜정
226	Dokdo Island is Ours 독도는 우리 땅 Lee Kwang-hee 이광희
228	While Making a Living 살다가 보면 Lee Geun-bae 이근배
230	A Scenery of the Mountain Village 산골 풍경 Lee Myung-woo 이명우
232	A Love Song of Flowering Dewdrops 이슬꽃 연가 Lee Beom-dong 이범동
234	A Train Station Inside Me 내 안의 역 Lee Byung-yeon 이병연
236	Snowflakes Blooming like Flowers in Winter 겨울 눈꽃 피다 Lee Bo-young 이보영

Contents

238   The Forest in May 오월의 숲 **Lee Bong-woo 이봉우**
240   The Drunken Sea 술에 취한 바다 **Lee Sang-jin 이생진**
242   Roses 장미 **Lee Soon-ock 이순옥**
244   A Streak of Tears 눈물 한 줄기만 **Lee Soon-Ja 이순자**
246   A Proposal of Marriage 구혼 **Lee Seung-ha 이승하**
248   Toxic Smog from Factory Chimneys 굴뚝의 노출 **Lee Young-kyoung 이영경**
250   Spring Days Are Special 봄날은 특별하다 **Lee Young-mi 이영미**
252   Azaleas 영산홍 **Lee Young-ae 이영애**
254   Folding Clothes 빨래를 개며 **Lee Ok-jin 이옥진**
256   The Ocean 바다 **Lee En-song 이은송**
258   Maidens in Spring 봄 처녀 **Lee Eui-young 이의영**
260   A Song for April 4월의 노래 **Lee In-ae 이인애**
262   Dandelions 민들레 **Lee Je-woo 이제우**
264   Rain in Spring 봄비 **Lee Ju-sig 이주식**
266   Farming 농사 **Lee Joon-hee 이준희**
268   On a Day like This 이런 날도 있다 **Lee Chang-sik 이창식**
270   A Nest for Birds 새집 **Lee Cheol-woo 이철우**
272   A Path by the River 강변 오솔길 **Lee Han-jae 이한재**
274   Asking Pardon 사죄謝罪 **Lee Hyang-ah 이향아**
276   My Mother Filling Up My Mind 어머니가 차오른다 **Lee Hyun-kyung 이현경**

278	Daffodils 수선화 **Lee Hye-sook 이혜숙**
280	If Love Gets Thicker 사랑이 짙어지면 **Yi Ho-yeon 이호연**
282	A Storage of Sorrow 슬픔의 창고 **Lee Hyo 이 효**
284	A Journey of Life 삶의 여정 **Lee Hee-bok 이희복**
286	Me, Being Pacified 나, 어르기 **Lim Bo-Seon 임보선**
288	Rain and Coffee 비와 커피 **Im So-ri 임소리**
290	Taegeukgi of Independence 광복의 태극기 **Yim Choong-bin 임충빈**
292	A Dream in Spring 봄꿈 **Lim Ha-cho 임하초**
294	The First Name 첫 이름 **Jang jin-ju 장진주**
296	Mt. Baekdu 백두산 **Chang Hae-ik 장해익**
298	Food 밥 **Jeon Min 전 민**
300	Bibimbob, Traditional Korean Meal 비빔밥 **Jun Yeoung-mo 전영모**
302	A Flower of Love 사랑의 꽃 **Jun Jong-moon 전종문**
304	The Wind Blowing at the Crater Lake 천지天池의 바람 **Jeon ji-myeong 전지명**
306	Seeing through a Dewdrop as a Magnifying Glass 이슬방울 돋보기로 들여다보니 **Jung soon-young 정순영**
308	A Broken Clock 고장 난 시계 **Cheong young-lye 정영례**
310	Everyone Becomes a Poet in Autumn 가을은 누구나 시인입니다 **Jeong Yeong-sook 정영숙**
312	COVID 19, I Ask for Your Return to Where You Came from

Contents

	코로나19, 조기 귀환을 빌다 Jung Yong-kyu 정용규
314	My Wife Became a Bird 새가 된 아내 Jung Jung-nam 정정남
316	Hangeul, Launched into the sky 한글, 쏘아 올리다 Jeong Hae-ran 정해란
318	Pain 통증痛症 Cho Kyu-soo 조규수
320	Coming out as a Flower 꽃이 되어 나오더라 Cho Duk-haee 조덕혜
322	The Mind of a Woman 여심 Jo Mi-ryeng 조미령
324	Going Beyond the Walls between South and North Korea 남과 북 장벽을 넘어서 Cho Young-mi 조영미
326	Mountains 산 Cho Byung-moo 조병무
328	People of Azaleas 진달래 민족 Cho Hae 조 해
330	The Meaning of Love 사랑의 의미意味 Chu Kwang-il 주광일
332	A Fugue of the Ocean 바다 둔주곡遁走曲 Ju Won-kyu 주원규
334	About my Hometown 내 고향은요 Jee Eun-kyung 지은경
336	It's Time to Brush with Love 사랑을 칠할 시간 Chae Ja-kyung 채자경
338	The Words of Reeds 갈대의 말씀 Choi kye-sik 최계식
340	The Ocean in Spring 봄 바다 Choi Young-hee 최영희
342	Blooming Flowers 꽃을 피우다 Choi Ihn-seok 최인석
344	The Sound of Opening the Dawn 새벽을 여는 소리 Choi Choon 최 춘
346	A Lunar Halo 달무리 Ha Gab-soo 하갑수

348 The Ocean As It Alway Has Been 늘 바다인 것을 **Han Ki-hong 한기홍**

350 Sitting in Front of a Tea Cup
찻잔을 앞에 두고 **Han Seong-geun 한성근**

352 Large Snowflakes 함박눈 **Hur Man-gil 허만길**

354 Snail 달팽이 **Heo Hyung-man 허형만**

356 Pretty Pebbles 예쁜 조약돌이 **Hong Kyung-ja 홍경자**

358 Gwanghwamun Square is Becoming a Hot Place
광화문 광장은 뜨고 있네요 **Hong In-sook 홍인숙**

360 Autumn 가을 **Hong Jung-gi 홍중기**

362 The Time I Spent with My Love
내 여자와의 시간 **Hwang Sun-ho 황선호**

364 Everything's Fine 괜찮아, 괜찮아 **Hwang Ok-rye 황옥례**

366 Dokdo Island 독도 **Hwang Ju-cheol 황주철**

K-POETRY
Getting on the Wings of Peace

Sunlight

It came all the way in a stride
from 150 million km away
and embraced water drops
dangling to the blade
before it ascends to the lake in the sky

Over the heads
of lovers
it sends back misty rain
For the trees
and flowers
it becomes a hearty friend

Turning water drops into pouring rain
the sunlight sent away my beloved one
to a place far, far away
and I cried
sobbing my heart out
following the bier being carried to the grave

Kang Bong-hwan
Member of The Korean Writers Association. Currently, Personnel business management consultant & Senior examiner of British Standards Institute

햇빛

일억오천만 킬로미터를
한걸음에 달려와
풀잎에 매달린
물방울들을 품고
하늘 호수로 올라갔습니다.

연인들
머리 위에
안개비를 내려주시고
꽃
나무들에게는
반가운 친구 되더니

작달비로 변해
내 사랑한 이를
먼… 곳으로 보냈습니다.
님은
서럽게 서럽게 울며
상여 따라갑니다.

강봉환
한국문인협회 회원,
현)경영컨설트 인사관리,
영국표준협회
선임심사원.

A Small House of Mine

I love a small house of mine
where the sunlight floods in to the veranda facing the south
I see the lovely sunset through the window in the kitchen
While little kids were becoming grown-ups
and a little kitten was getting older
seedlings also have grown into mature plants

I can see the blue sky where cool breeze blows from
at my own little oasis surrounded by skyscrapers
and I write poems containing the scent of orchid flowers
in a languid afternoon when my cat is sleeping
sometimes with cicadas breaking the quietude of the day
With all these surrounding me, I love a small house of mine

Kang Elly
Poet, novelist and lyricist. CEO of The Garden of Ellis' Poetry. Published poetry book, *The Only One Dream*

나의 작은 집

나는 나의 작은 집을 사랑하네
남쪽 베란다 깊숙이 햇살이 들어오고
부엌 창으로 예쁜 석양이 보이는 집
어린아이들이 자라 멋진 어른이 되고
아기고양이 나이를 먹는 동안
작은 모종들이 튼실한 나무로 자랐네

푸른 하늘이 보이고 시원한 바람 부는
마천루로 둘러싸인 작은 오아시스
꽃대궁 올린 난 향기 가득한 시를 쓰고
고양이 낮잠 자는 나른한 오후
매미 울음소리 한낮의 정적을 깨뜨리는
나의 작은 집을 사랑하네

강에리
소설가·작사가·시인,
엘리스의시가있는
정원 대표,
시집 『단 하나의 꿈』

Time

Despite your will looking to leave me
I swear I wouldn't let you go easily
for you are my best friend
But saying good bye, you always turn around
with the shadow, making me feel wistful all the time
Despite all the efforts to hold you with my arms
you pull yourself out of my hands
and run ahead of me, moving faster than I expect
like a horse without reins put on
I like to kiss you, cherishing every each day
making you stay by my side quietly
catching and releasing you
little by little and step by step
You are the companion of silence

Kang Yeoung-deok
Poet. Steering committee member of Korea Sinmunye Literature Association. Awarded Esprit Literature Prize and more. Published poetry book *A Channel of Time*

세월

떠나려 하여도
쉽게 보낼 수 없는
단짝 같은 친구이건만
끝내 이별을 고하고 뒤돌아서서
아쉬운 눈시울 적시는 그림자
품어도 꼭 껴안아도
어느새 빠져나와
늘 나의 의지보다
앞장서서 달리기만 하는
고삐 풀린 말
소중히 하루하루 입맞춤하며
조용히 내 곁에 두고
조금씩, 서서히
풀었다 낚았다 하고 싶은
침묵의 동반자

강영덕
한국신문예문학회
운영위원,
에스프리문학상 외,
시집 『시간의 채널』 외.

An Icicle

In the warm sunshine snow melting water is running down
Our warm love and fruitful cold wave being brought together
for the love of sunlight gradually add delightful tears
while jealous Jack Frost is making us more beautiful

You and I as pure as crystal
gain weight, growing downward in big love
Our bodies get thick glowing at every roof-end tile
like a rainbow with the dream projected in the sunlight

A roof piled up with white snow
displays a sign of our warm love
to General Winter being jealous of us
with the bearing of the Trinity, 'snow, water, cold'

If the Jack Frost leaves us,
where should you and I go to?
Getting closer to the end of a rich life,
we will shed icy tears until we finally return, falling to the soil

*roof-end tiles : Tiles located at the end of the eaves

Kang Chang-seok
Board member of The Korean Writers Association & Gangnam Poetry Literature Association.
Awarded Korea Literature Association Prize and more

고드름

따스한 햇살 눈물雪水 흘러내리고
우리 사랑 따뜻함과 한파의 결실
햇빛 사랑에 겨워 눈물은 조금씩 더해 가고
질투하는 동장군 우리를 더욱 아름답게
합니다

수정같이 순수한 너와 나
아래로 사랑을 살찌우고
막새기와* 골마다 커가는 우리들의 몸
햇살에 투영된 영롱한 빛 무지개의 꿈

백설 소복이 쌓인 지붕
따뜻한 사랑의 애액
우리를 시샘하는 동장군
雪, 水, 寒 삼위일체 결실

동장군 물러가면
너와 나 어디로 가야 하는가
풍요로운 삶은 찔끔찔끔 눈물 흘리며
낙빙되어 흙으로 돌아가리라.

* 막새기와 : 처마 끝 기와

강창석
한국문학협회·강남포에트
리문학회 이사
한국문학협회 문학대상 외.

A Dandelion's Territory

A dandelion is like a spacecraft
having landed on the weedy field

Growing in a strange area unlike the hometown
it drinks tap water affecting the complexion of the face
making it forget the dialect it was born with

Suffering from monthly payment for rental home
until it finally bought its own residence
it has been going through hard times

With its fine root of life
stretching carefully into the ground
a dandelion keeps dreaming for its own territory

Go Geum-seok
Vice-president of Seoul Future Arts Association. Member of Korea Music Copyright Association. Published poetry book *Buds of the Universe*

민들레 영토

민들레는 하얀 우주선
무성한 잡초밭에 착륙했다

고향 떠나 낯선 동네
수돗물 먹고 얼굴색도 변하고
사투리도 잊어버렸다

보금자리 마련 위해
월세방 전세방 시달리며
집 한 채 장만하던 사연도 많다

실뿌리 인생
조심스레 뻗으며
민들레 영토를 꿈꾼다.

고금석
서울미래예술협회 부회장
음악저작권협회 회원
저서 『우주의 새싹』 외.

Cape Seopjikoji

Ponies on the hill
wagging their tails
awaken romantic feelings inside me

Yellow mustard flowers
fully blooming all over the place
make my mind sway following the flowers

Along the curved seashore
at the remote area where even the wind hides
I can smell the fragrance soaking my mind

At the tip of the cape
protruding like a nose
I blow away the hardships of life in the ocean breeze

Feeling like I am here in the hill of happiness

Ko Eung-nam
Poet, essayist, painter. Vice-president of Insadong Poets Association & President of Korea Arts Newspaper

섭지코지

언덕배기 조랑말
꼬리를 흔들며
타고 싶은 낭만을 깨우네

노란 유채꽃
천지에 흐드러져
내 마음도 따라 일렁이네

구부러진 해안을 따라
바람도 숨어버린 한적한 곳에
고운 향기는 내 마음 적시네

비죽 튀어나온
코의 끄트머리에서
세파에 흐린 마음
맑은 해풍에 날려 보내니

여기가 바로 행복 동산이라네

고응남
시인·수필가·화가,
인사동시인협회 부회장,
대한예술신문 총재.

Father's Fan Air Blower

Sometimes I make a fat cow and a brazier in red

Early in the evening, my father set fire in the fire pit
From a large iron kettle wherein dried grasses, rice straws
and lots of rice husks were being cooked came pleasant smell
of cow fodder, swirling around the room next to the main gate

Having extended metal air outlet of fan air blower
and blowing air into the mouth of fire pit make dying embers
alive and burn the logs fiercely enough to make the kettle boil
with steam

My father used to put the hands on the warm spot in my granny's room to check on the temperature, and it was like a duty for him

While the cow was sticking the tongue out and rolling it
around the large bowl full of fodder, my father patted
the cow's back with his hands getting thick in the joints,
watching the cow chewing the cud, blinking its big eyes

My father is still alive as the air of fan blower

Ko Hwa-soon
Made literary debut through *Wolgan Munhak*. Graduated from JoongAng Univ. Member of The Korean Writers Association. Former general director of Gwangju Writers Association.

아버지의 풍로

가끔은 살찐 소와 붉은 화덕을 만든다

이른 저녁 군불을 지피던 아버지
마른풀과 잘게 썬 짚 위에
딩기가루 듬뿍 뿌린 가마솥에서
소여물 익는 구수한 냄새 행랑채를
휘돌았다

아궁이 깊이 연통을 늘이고 풍로를
돌리면 사그라지던 불씨는 금세
장작개비를 달구어 놀란
가마솥 눈물을 흘린다

할머니방 아랫목에 손을 넣어 대충
방의 온기를 가늠하던 아버지의 시간

여물통 가득히 쇠죽을 퍼주는 바가지에
긴 혀를 날름거리는 소의 등 어루만지던
아버지의 굵은 손마디
큰 눈을 깜박이며 새김질하는 외양간

아버지의 풍로는 바람으로 살아있다

고화순
《월간문학》등단,
중앙대학교 졸업,
한국문협 회원,
광주문협 사무국장 역임.

Your Smile

Seeing you smile
makes everybody happy

Let's talk in warm and friendly way
greeting everyone with a smile

Let's try to see the bright side only
of the things around us

Although they have thorns
roses also bloom on the same stems
Let's appreciate the beauty of roses

Kwak Kwang-tack
Advisory member of Domgjak Writers Association. Auditor of Korea Senior Citizen's Rights Association. Published poetry book *Hometown of the Mind*

당신의 미소

당신의 미소를 보면
누구나 마음이 즐겁다

부드러운 말로
웃으면서 인사하자

항상 사물의 밝은 면만
보도록 노력하자

장미에도 가시가 있다
가시에 꽃이 피는 것에
감사하자

곽광택
동작문협 고문,
한국노년인권협회 감사,
시집 『마음의 고향』 외

The Cold Snap in Spring

A red plum flower
comes blearily in sight

The lofty appearance blooming in snow
takes people's breath away

All of sudden, the cold snap coming to us
crushes the harbinger of spring
freezing the flowers in envy
making me sad
enjoying itself with cold heart
while spring is comforting bees and butterflies

Oh, you lingering winter yet to stay,
you are so unscrupulous
You should live not to be blamed for later
if you know the seasonal change is at hand

Kwak Jong-chul
Vice president of Korean War Literature Association. Awarded Literature & Artists Prize.
Published poetry book *Flowers Blooming on Qyestion Marks* and more

꽃샘추위

한 떨기 홍매화꽃이
게슴츠레하게 뜬 눈에 들온다

눈 속에서 피운 고결한 자태
보는 이를 더 열광케 한다

봄의 전령을 뭉개버리고
뜻밖에 시샘하는 날씨
꽃은 슬프다
나도 슬프다
겨울은 아직도 흥얼거리고
봄은 벌 나비를 토닥인다

머물고 싶은 야윈 동장군아,
너 그렇게 살지 말라
그래도 욕은 안 먹고 살아야지
세상이 곧 바뀔 텐데

곽종철
한국전쟁문학회 부회장,
문학예술인상 외
시집『물음표에
피는 꽃』외.

I Like You Being a Rock

I like you being a rock
looking like a good general

I like you being reserved
keeping things inside you

I like you being trustworthy
having such a generous heart

Kwon Kyou-ho
Poet, artist. Board member of Korea Sinmunye
Literature Association

바위라서 좋다

네가 바위라서 좋다
듬직한 장군 같아 좋다

입이 있어도 함부로 말하지 않는
천금보다 무거운 입이어서 좋다

그저 믿음직스러운
큰 가슴이어서 네가 좋다

권규호
시인·예술인,
한국신문예문학회
이사.

A Class of Sheep

The Palgong mountain range
with valleys high and low

Bumpy uphill road
uneven with stubborn stones

Whispering
during the class

Beautiful sunset gives
a congratulation

Kwon Dae-ja
Former vice-president of Daegu Writers Association. Awarded Korea Children's Literature Writers Prize. Published poetry book *Stories of Nature in Andong*

양들의 수업

팔공산맥
높고 낮은 계곡

울퉁불퉁한
오르막 길

소곤소곤
수업 중에

고운 노을이
축하하네

권대자
대구문인협회 부회장
역임, 한국아동문학 42
회 작가상 외,
저서 『경북 안동 자연이
주는 이야기』 외.

Magnolia

If you see me while just turning around, you can go past me lightly
Unless you would come and embrace me
you can just go away following the wind, passing by me

If you come here being carried by the fragrance in the wind
and you are not going away leaving footprints only
you may pacify me tired of coming a long way with lofty purity

I am here after a long trip, never forgetting the love you gave me
Please, embrace me with your heart
that will make me stay a little longer beside you

Even if I feel myself trembling at your hands
and fall silently on the ground, I won't blame you for that
Just make a promise
when spring comes again next year
you would come by here following the scent of mine
to caress me with your love so kind and tender

Kim Kyung-hee
Poet, essayist. Member of Korea Modern Poets Association. Published poetry book *Mugunghwa, Rose of Sharon, is in full bloom*

목련

언뜻 돌아보다 보신 거라면 스치듯
가셔도 됩니다
찾아와 보듬지 못할 거라면
부는 바람 따라 그냥 가셔도 됩니다

날리는 향에 이끌리어 오신
머무는 발길이 임이시라면
순백의 고귀함으로 먼 길 와줘 고맙다고
다독여 주소서

주신 사랑 못 잊어 멀고 먼 길 찾아 왔으니
임이여 조금만 더 머물다 갈 수 있게
보듬어 안아 주소서

주신 손길에 파르르 떨리어
소리 없이 진다 한들 야속치 않으리니
임이여 기약하소서
이 봄 지나 새봄 오면
날리는 향기에 발길 머물고
한없이 어루만져 사랑하겠노라고

김경희
시인·수필가, 한국현대
시협 회원,
시집 『무궁화 꽃이 피었
습니다』 외.

A Natural Burial

Me
I am not here
During the days I had lived
as a young woman for a short period
your father changed my name
calling me "yeobo"*

Having lost my own name
I had to live a whole life
as a wooden pillar to support family bloodline

Even after I died
there is no me
but a tree root I became

* "yeobo" in Korean refers to a wife, meaning darling, honey, sweetheart in English

---

Kim Kwan-sik
Poet, literary critic. Ph. D. in literature. Member of The Korean Writers Association. Published many books of poetry, children's poems, criticism

수목장 樹木葬

나
없다.
젊은 날
여자로 살았던 짧은 순간
내 이름조차 네 아비가
"여보"로 바꿔 놓았다.

이름을 잊어버리고
평생을 핏줄기 잇는
기둥으로 살아왔다.

죽어서도
나 없다
나무뿌리가 되었다.

김관식
시인·문학평론가·
문학박사,
한국문협 회원,
시집·동시집·평론집
다수.

A Prologue
—A New World

Greet a dawn starting a new day
Embrace the glaring sun rising
Plant a new dream for knowledge

Inhale the radiating sunlight
With your smart brain and skills
Cultivate dexterity for the future

Give fertilizer of real wisdom
With high-technology developed in sweat
Make the advanced world

Putting knowledge well riped in the soul
For the achievement shining like new stars
Make your life worthwhile

Kim Kwan-hyung
Professor at Myungji Univ. Advisory member of Korea Sinmunye Literature Association.
Published poetry book *A Mirro of the Journey Worthwhile* and more

서시
– 새누리

새날 뜨는 새벽을 열어라
솟아오르는 햇덩이를 품고
햇 꿈을 지식 밭에 심어라

찬란한 날빛 숨을 마셔라
예리한 두뇌 뛰어난 솜씨로
진한 재주를 길러라

참된 슬기의 거름을 주어라
땀이 배인 높은 기술 거두어
앞선 누리 만들어라

영근 알음 넋 속에 담아라
새롬이 별처럼 빛나는 이룸
보람찬 삶에 주어라

김관형
명지대 교수, 한국신문
예문학회자문위원,
시집 『보람 깃든 여로의
거울』 외.

Answers to Love

More I love
I see love is everything
Beyond any expression
Love exists
Despite of knowing what love is like
Love doesn't mean any less
With the words not enough to describe
Love is ineffable
In spite of doubting how long it would continue
Love lasts forever
More you love, more it adds up
Love multiplies
Love is the question with no answer
Love itself is both the question and the answer
The more you love, the deeper you falls in love

Kim Dae-eung
Poet, pastor. Member of The Korean Writers Association. Published poetry book *Mungkeul* (2023)

사랑에 대한 답

사랑할수록
사랑은 사랑입니다
무슨 말로 표현해도 부족한
사랑입니다
이제 그 마음 다 알았다 해도
사랑입니다
표현할 말이 부족한 이 세상 단어
사랑입니다
언제까지 사랑할 수 있을까 하여도
사랑입니다
사랑은 사랑할수록 더 곱하기 되는
사랑입니다
사랑은 사랑이라는 말 외에 답이 없는
사랑입니다
사랑할수록 사랑은 사랑합니다

김대응
시인·목사, 한국문협
회원, 시집 『뭉클』

Magic Lily at Seonunsa Temple

The foliage never sees the flower
for it dies before the flower appears
As if bursting into tears suppressed for so long
bundles of flamboyant flowers bloom
unfurling their petals, resisting to be lonely
With single-minded devotion towards a lover
magic lily watches its own shadow
laid over the waterway of Dosolchun stream
Longing for the lover
getting hardened inside the flower stalk
makes the flowers bloom in bloody color
looking like a fire flaring up in the fresh verdure

Kim Do-yeon
Poet, painter. Vice-president of The Korean Writers Association at Jongro Branch. Published poetry book *Flowers That Don't Fall* and more

선운사의 상사화

잎은 꽃을 못 보고
꽃은 잎을 못 보다가
참았던 붉은 울음 토해내는가
외롭지 않으려 화려한 꽃잎들
무리 지어 피었는가
님 향한 일편단심 한恨이 되어
도솔천 물길따라 드리운
제 그림자 바라보며
애틋한 마음들이 응어리진 그리움
꽃대 속내에 담았다가
타오르는 진한 핏빛
녹음 사이로 붉게 빛나네

김도연
시인·화가, 한국문협종
로지부 부회장,
시집 『지지 않는 꽃』 외.

A Meal

Having a meal every day
without skipping it by any means

But if I miss it once in a while by chance
it makes my guts roar like a thunderstorm

It would be a lot better if we don't need you

For both the rich and the powerful
you make them cry
you make them laugh
you make them live
you make them die

Shaking upside down
every soul alive in this world
you are the most powerful authority

Kim Myung-ja
Poet, poetry recitor. President of The Korean Writers Association at Jechun Branch. Awarded Park Wha-mok Literature Prize and more. Published poetry book *A Happy Person* and more

밥

날마다 먹고 또 먹어도
단 한 번도 물러날 줄 모르고

어쩌다 하루라도 빠지는 날이면
꼬르륵 꾸르륵 천둥 치듯 뱃속을
뒤흔드는 너

아예 없었으면 참 좋겠는데…

부자나 권력자나
너로 인해 울고
너로 인해 웃고
네가 있어 살고
네가 있어 죽는다

살아 움직이는 모든 영혼을
뒤집고 흔드는 너는
지구상의 최고 권력자.

김명자
시인·시낭송가,
한국문협제천지회장,
박화목문학상 외,
시집 『행복한 사람』 외.

Dark Shades of May

Devastating news on TV reminds me of the Korean War
Death of family of the same blood turns tears into blood
Grieving the loss in explosion of bombs is televised on the screen

Human dignity is destroyed and missing right now
At the border of life and death people are suffering
With no prospect to the peace imminently found

As if walking in the mine field all day long in the heart
Feeling trapped in the tunnel of life as dark as it gets
Ukrainians see the country become a river full of cries

On the day felt sorrowful with the broken heart in silence
getting bruises all over, the greens yet flourish in May
and I desperately hope you to laugh as in good old days

Kim Min-jeong
Sijo poet. Ph.D. in literature. Vice-president of he Korean Writers Association. Awarded THe Writers Prize of The Korean Writers Association. Published the collection of sijo *Dream in the Land* and more

오월의 그늘 (시조)

초극의 참상 앞에 6.25가 떠오른다
피붙이 목숨에는 눈물도 피가 된다
화면을 빠져나오는 저 포탄의 몸부림

인간의 존엄성이 실종된 지금 여기
죽음을 코앞에 둔 삶의 경계에서
막막한 평화의 주소 어디에서 찾을까

마음의 지뢰밭은 온종일 걷고 있다
생의 한가운데 터널처럼 캄캄하다
정지된 우크라이나 울음이 된 강이다

고요를 뒤흔드는 침묵만이 서러운 날
피멍 든 오월에도 물오르는 초록처럼
간절히 너를 부른다 예전처럼 웃자꾸나

김민정
시조시인·문학박사,
한국문협 부이사장,
한국문협작가상 외,
시조집 『지상의 꿈』
외.

Waves

The rocks slapped across the face kick back the waves
startling the sun to hide in somewhere

The clouds getting thicker and darker run away
leaving everything behind as if taking off hurriedly

Waiting for the morning after the moon and the stars disappeared
we all run to find how the crashing sound is made in the shore

With the sun hidden in the dark during the night rising again
we see the waves swashing back abashedly at ebb tide

Kim Baik-kyung
Board member of International PEN, Korea Center. Awarded Baekdusan Literature Prize and more. Published books including *Let's Go to the Ocean, Tomorrow* and more

파도

뺨 맞고 성난 바위가 파도를 걷어차니
흉흉한 그 기세에 해님조차 숨는구나

구름도 낯이 변해 허둥지둥 도망갈 때
등짐도 다 버리고 뺑소니치는구나

달도 별도 사라지고 아침을 기다리다
쫘아악 급한 소리에 모두가 뛰었는데

숨은 해님 방긋이 얼굴 살짝 내미니
파도가 계면쩍어 스르르릉 도망간다

김백경
국제펜한국본부 이사,
백두산문학상 외,
저서 『바다로 가자 내일
은』 외.

Yes, As of Today

Bursting cherry blossoms outside the window
fall even before spring message is conveyed
leaving us all behind
dancing and fluttering
so lighly in the wind
Like the petals of cherry blossoms
old people fall, ending their lives
with the stories of blooming and falling
Flowers will bloom again where they fell
after they survive the long, cold winter
Even though we are not sure
if we can see the dazzling moment of a life
or even if we are sure we will see the moment
all that matters is
we are shining as of today

Kim Bong-Kyum
Poet, lawyer. Member of The Korean Writers Association & Korea Christian Writers Association

그래, 오늘

거실 창밖엔 벚꽃 만발滿發,
그 소식 다 전하기도 전에
벗어 던지고 떠나길,
가벼이 나풀나풀
쉬이도 흩날린다
꽃이파리처럼,
노생老生들 분분히 떠나는 소식마저
꽃피고 지는 얘기와 헝클어진다
꽃 진 자리 또 필 테지만
긴 겨울고개를 넘어 견뎌내야 한다
다시, 만개滿開의 화사함을
마주할 수나 있을는지
앞으로 더 황홀한 날이 있다 해도
그래,
오늘 이대로 눈부시다.

김봉겸
시인·변호사,
한국문협 회원,
한국크리스천문학가
협회 회원.

Royal Azaleas Blooming in Clusters

Where can we find such a beautiful cluster of flowers
like candlelights shown in the peaceful protest?
They are spectacular to see

At this time of the year, former comfort women
wearing skirts
rush out to everywhere all at once
making protests as they do, standing upside down

They want to let people know
their body was sacred and beautiful, too,
like other women's

Over the skirts hanging down below
exposing underpants with traces of the first period
those protesters standing upside down
make a river full of dark pink clusters of flowers

Kim Sang-cheol
Member of Korea Modern Poets Association. Awarded the Best Prize at National Writing Contest in 2014. Published poetry book *If Spring Comes*

철쭉꽃 무리

저렇게 예쁘고 평화로운 촛불 시위가
어디 또 있을까
장관이다 장관

이때가 되면 가엾은 위안부 처녀들은
곳곳에 한꺼번에 몰려나와
치마 입은 채,
물구나무서서 저리 시위를 한다

자기들의 성性도 마찬가지로
성스럽고 아름다웠음을
알리기 위해서다

치마가 머리쪽에 내려간 속바지마다
젖은 초경初經 물이 뚝뚝 떨어지도록
거꾸로 선 시위대들이
진분홍 꽃무리 강을 이루고 있다

김상철
한국현대시인협회 회원,
2014전국백일장
최우수상,
시집 『봄이 오면』 외.

A Dewdrop

A tear of the star dangling at the severed string of spider web

No matter how fast and acceleratingly it is shaken

Its gesture shows it is traveling in space, holding the air tightly

Kim Su-yeoun
Board member of International PEN, Korea Center. Awarded Oversea Literature Prize of The Korean Writers Association. Published poetry book *The Yard in Green*

이슬 한 방울 (시조)

끊어진 거미줄에 매달린 별의 눈물

휘모리장단으로 아무리 흔들어도

허공을 움켜쥔 채로 우주여행 몸짓이다

김수연
국제펜한국본부 이사,
한국문협해외문학상 외,
시집 『초록의 뜰』 외.

Song of Spring

With gentle smiles
Adonis flowers burst to bloom lightly
With the spring coming
The buds of witch hazel grow to pop up

Sprouting leaves of magic lilies stealthily turn up,
Sticking out their yellowish green faces

Every branch having trembled with reddish skin color
While enduring the cold wind with warm breath only
Now regains the strength with the spring coming

With the energetic spirit of blue dragon
Everything comes singing the song of fulfilling spring

Kim Ae-ran
Poet, essayist, travel writer. Awarded Hwang Jin-hee Literature Prize. Published poetry book *Gemstone with the Similar Color of the Sky*

봄 노래

미소 머금은
복수초 톡 톡 터지는 소리
풍년화 봄소식에
꽃망울 팡팡 터지는 소리

상사화 잎들도 슬그머니
쏙쏙 내미는 연둣빛 얼굴

가지마다 붉은빛 감도는 피부
찬바람 호호 손을 떨던 가지들은
봄을 끌어 올리며 쑥쑥

기운찬 청룡 기운으로
충만한 봄 노래로 온다

김애란
시인·수필가·여행작가
황진이문학상 최우수상
시집 『하늘빛 닮은 원석으로』 외.

The Spirits of the Olympics and Korea

With all attentions of the people focused on the Seine River in 2024
Paris gets as hot as the temperatures of the earth

The young athletes from all over the world challenging for human limits
gathered with passion competing for the the Olympic medals
at the Square of Anvalide where Napoleon is buried

Making efforts with passionate enthusiasm and devotion
Korean players won the gold medals in shooting tournament, fencing and archery;
especially in the women's team event, they won ten consecutive gold medals, which made us feel proud of Korean teams in other nation's admiration

With Taegukki, our national flag, fluttering high in the sky of Paris
strong culture of Korea too widely spread to the world
embroidering the hearts of the people with beautiful heritage of our ancestors

Watching the athletes having competed fiercely in the Olympics embrace and encourage each other with the spirits of the Olympics after the events
I wish there could be no more wars in this beautiful world full of humanity, aspiring for world peace with the spirits as we see from the Olympics!

Kim Young-soon
Poet, essayist, novelist. Secretary-general of Sinmunye Literature Association. Awarded the 11th Esprit Literature Prize and more

올림픽 정신과 대한민국

2024년 세느강에 모인 세계인의 눈과 귀
뜨거워진 지구만큼이나 달궈진 파리

인간의 한계에 도전하는 세계 젊은이들
열정이 모여 함께하는 올림픽 잔치
앵발리드 광장 나폴레옹이 묻힌 곳

김영순
시인·수필가·소설가
신문예문학회 사무국장
제11회 에스프리문학상 외.

남녀불문 열정과 집념으로 흘린 땀방울
평화의 총 칼 활로 세상을 제패하고
세계가 부러워할 대한의 딸들
여자 양궁 올림픽 금메달 10연패 달성

파리 하늘 높이 휘날린 태극기
굳건히 다지는 코리아의 문화
세계로 세계로 아름답게 수놓고

격렬하게 겨루다가도 다시 얼싸안는
이기고 진이 서로 격려하는 올림픽 정신
세계인의 축제 평화의 정신 가득한
아름다운 지구촌에 전쟁은 이제 그만!

The Sounds of Rain Pouring at My Parents' Home

The sounds of rain pouring through the night
make me stay awake

At the birthday of my father stricken in years
the absence of his oldest son was felt
as much as his affection to the son

How much has he loved his son since childhood?

With the dark clouds lying at the mountain ridge
the rain pouring through the night makes me sad

This pouring rain might be the tears
of my mother looking down from the heaven
the empty place of the oldest son

Kim Young-yup
Poet. MA in social welfare. Board member of Insadong Poets Association. Awarded Hwang jin-hee Literature Prize.

친정집 빗소리

밤새 쏟아지는 빗소리에
잠 못 이룬다

연로하신 아버지 생신 때
함께 하지 못한
맏아들의 빈 자리는 크기만 하다

김영엽
인사동시인협회 이사,
황진이문학상,
사회복지석사졸업.

어려서부터 얼마나 애지중지하셨던 아들
인가

저 멀리 산등성이에 검은 구름 가득하고
밤새도록 줄기차게 내리는 저 빗소리는

맏아들의 빈 자리를 내려다보시며
정녕 하늘나라에서 흘리신
어머니의 눈물인가보다

March

March, if I call for you
you make the stream flow loud and clear
underneath the icy valley that has been frozen

Wind, if I call for you
you blow into the heart with a gentle smile
unlike the lover once having turned around coldly

Flowers, if I call for you
you show your faces shyly before we notice
bringing forth the petals of azalea flowers unfurled yet
growing, though, cracking the hard surface of branches

Longing inside me, if I call for you
you fly up in the sky at a distance
following a piece of cloud
making me feel touched in my heart

Kim Young-weol
Poet, essayist. Former president of The Korean Writers Association at Dobong Branch.
Published poetry book *Overall, Our Life Has been Good*

삼월

삼월이여, 소리 내어 부르면
얼음 밑 숨죽여 흐르던 계곡물
대답하듯 콸콸콸 거린다

바람이여, 소리내어 부르면
그동안 돌아선 임 같던 쌀쌀한 바람결
살랑대는 웃음으로 가슴에 안긴다

꽃이여, 소리내어 부르면
어느새 딱딱한 가지를 찢고
젖망울 같은 진달래 꽃잎
수줍게 얼굴을 내민다

그리움이여, 소리내어 부르면
가슴 한 켠 알 수 없이 뭉클하여
먼데 하늘 가
한 조각 구름을 쫓는다

김영월
시인·수필가, 한국문협
도봉지부 회장 역임,
저서 「그래도 괜찮은
삶」 외.

Weight of Time

On the ridges cracked by drought between rice paddies
grow a handful of mugwort
On the green onion, chili, lettuce trimmed with coarse hands
well up a drop of tear and then another piteously

Even long after the market closed
the warmth in life stays there
wriggling under the hazy lamplight
while an old woman with a bent back is groaning
revealing the weight of despair dangling down to the earth
breaking the silence of the alley

Sprouts of hopes grow in silence
from deep down under the soil with dreams
burning like fire even in the forlorn market closed
keeping the beauty of daily life, enduring the hardship of life,
like the old woman whose eyes are shining, waiting for the last sale
The embers of hopes are still alive overcoming the weight of poverty

About this alley, this market, this moment
I will sing a song
to shed light on people living in joys and sorrows
their endless waiting and hopes
sustaining their lives under the hazy lamplight

Kim Wang-sik
Essayst, literary critic. Former teacher at Osan High School. Founder& Administrator of Chungram Gifted Students Institute. Awarded the grand prize in criticism at Korea Literature Newspaper's Contest.

시간의 무게

가뭄에 쩍쩍 갈라진 논두렁
비집고 나온 쑥 한 줌
투박한 손길 애처로이 다듬는 파,
고추, 상추 위로 눈물방울 하나,
또 하나 고이네

파장罷場한 지 오래
희미한 가로등 아래 꿈틀대는
삶의 온기
허리 굽은 노파의 신음 소리
땅에 닿을 듯 매달린 절망의 무게를
드러내며 골목 안 고요를
깨뜨린다

희망의 싹은 조용히, 아주 조용히
흙 속 깊이 자리잡고 있다
시장의 쓸쓸함 속에도 불꽃처럼 피어오르는 소박한 꿈들,
묵묵히 버티는 일상의 아름다움
떨이를 기다리는 노파의 눈빛
가난의 무게 이겨낼 작은 희망의 불씨가 여전히 살아 숨쉬네

이 골목, 이 시장, 이 순간들이
서민의 시린 애환
끝없는 기다림과 희망을
가로등 아래 희미하게나마 비추는
이 골목의 노래로 남기네

김왕식
수필가·문학평론가,
전)서울오산고등학교
교사, 한국문학신문
공모전 평론부분 대상.

Green Tea in Dream

In a thick fog from the river surrounding Mt. Hwalseong fortress
flying down to Mt. Mongjung in a dream
where five Taoist Hermits were believed to play Go game
swallows wake up the tea field
singing, chirp, chirp, chirp
upon which young tea leaves grow
in the furrows named as blue dragon area
Having picked up the baby green tea leaves
tumbling and roasting them nine times in the heat
with the sounds of gentle crackling, pops and hisses
we can finally enjoy a new green tea with a smile
After drinking the first green tea, you feel the rising morning star
after drinking the green tea seven times,
you can feel the light of morning sun shining in your heart

* bright early morning sun shin

Kim Young-kook
The head of Local History Research Center in Boseung. The 19th president of Jeonnam Writers Association. Published poetry book *Jhwaja in the Tea Forrest*

꿈속의 차

보성강 안개가 감싼 활성산성
다섯 신선 바둑 두는 꿈속 몽중산을
제비들이 찾아와서 깨우면
짹짹짹짹
차밭 청룡 이랑 가득
작설들이 솟아난다.
아침 햇살 머금은 찻순 따서
아홉 번 덖고 비비면
사그랑 사그라랑
대한 차인이 꿈꾸는 햇차가 웃는다.
첫 잔 한 모금에 샛별이 돋고
일곱 잔 마시면
가슴속 가득 깃밝이*가 퍼진다.

김용국
보성향토사연구소장,
제19대 전남문협회장
역임, 저서 『차 숲에서
지화자』

A Realization

In the world
there are many things to forgive in others

In the world
there is nothing I should forgive in others, though

Kim Yong-ok
Vice-president of International PEN, Korea Center. Awarded Korea Modern Poets Association Literature Prize. Published many poetry books and the collections of essays

각 覺

세상엔
용서해야 할 것이 많습니다.

세상엔
내가 용서해야 할 것이 없습니다.

김용옥
국제펜 부이사장
현대시문학상 외
시집과 수필집 다수.

Porcelain Jar

Carrying the moon on the head
come, then leave me as if you have never been here
If a wind-bell rings, hanging at the eaves of mountain temple you told me to think you have passed by me in the wind
Now I am standing with my hands put together in front of a paroda
when a lad in yellow clothes comes to me
pointing the mountain ridge in cloud and fog
resounding your voice inside me,
recommending to empty the mind, to keep the body open
encouraging me to fill my life with a variety of experiences
until my body born naked gets broken into pieces
for the life is meant to be so valuable
teaching me to free the mind slowly but surely
with the heart cleansed by sugared water from gigantic rocks,
all these making new joy keep popping up inside me

Kim Woon-hyang
Poet, novelist. Ph.D. in literature. Committee member of The Korean Writers Association. Awarded Peasant's Literature Prize. Published poetry book, *La Novia of the Cloud and more*

항아리

머리에 달을 이고
아니 오신 듯, 다녀가소서
산사의 처마 끝에 매달린 풍경 울리거든
바람결에 그님이 스쳐갔다 여기시라기에
천봉당 태흘탑 아래서 합장하노라니
노란 옷을 입은 소년이 나타나
운무 드리워진 능선을 가리키네
마음 한 곳을 비우고
몸 한 곳도 열어두기를
귀한 인연으로 빚어진 삶인데
알몸으로 와서 조각조각 깨질 때까지
골고루 채우고 비워보기를
큰 바위 속에서 흘러넘치는 감로수로
청정심 되어 시나브로 비우리라 하니
새로운 법열이 새록새록 밀려드네.

김운향
시인·소설가·문학박사,
한국문협 위원, 농민문
학상 대상.
시집 『구름의 라노비
아』 외.

Phrases Posted to Welcome Spring

Ipchundaegil*, Gunyangdakyung*
I got these two phrases back again to welcome spring
since I put the same phrases on the door last year

The phrases for the best wishes melt snow still lingering
sounding very close to my rusty ears with hope for rejuvenation
Nonetheless, rather than feeling delight in spring coming so soon
I find myself missing the time I have been waiting for spring so long

Getting older, I see the season change faster coming with quick steps
Despite complaints that time run fast as if violating the speed limit
I write 8 Chinese character for Ipchundaegil, Gunyangdakyung
and put them on the door in the figure of eight in Chinese letter
wearing my clothes adjusted to make a new hope fit for the year

---

* Ipchundaegil : this phrase written in Chines refers to "Good luck for spring"
* Gunyangdakyung : this phrase written in Chines refers to "May spring bring this family blessings and fill this home with lights"

Traditionally these phrases are posted on a door or a wall on the day of the onset to spring, hoping for good luck and blessing to the family

---

Kim Yoo-jo
Poet, novelist. Vice-president of International PEN, Korea Center. Professor emeritus at Konkuk Univ.(served as former vice-president)

시 입춘방

입춘대길 건양다경
지난해 입춘방 붙인 게 엊그제인데
새로 여덟 자를 받았다

축원 담은 따뜻한 글귀가 잔설을 녹이고
회춘의 희망가로 녹슨 귓전에 울리지만
금방 다시 온 반가움보다
오래 기다리던 시절이 더 그립다

나이 들며 맞이하는 모든 절기의 종종걸음
속도위반이라 투정 부리면서도
입춘대길 건양다경 여덟 글자
여덟팔자로 고이 붙이고
새 옷 옷깃 여미듯 새 소망을 다시 여민다

김유조
국제PEN한국본부 부
이사장, 건국대 명예
교수(부총장 역임),
저서 소설집 다수.

A Pond in the Sky

Looking up into the sky, missing the place
For a visit by riding on the cloud of longing

Sorrows overflowing the pond
Come down in drops
Soaking me like a heavy rain

How large the pond is in the sky, I wonder,
Everything of a life is contained in the pond
Every story of a life seems to be there swimming

The more I love, the wider the pond gets
With the flowers breathing and singing in love
A rainbow bridge is laid in my mind as always

Kim Eun-soo
Central committee member of Korea Modern Poets Association. CEO of Eungerm Sihak.
Published poetry book *A Pond in the Sky* and more

하늘 연못

보고 싶어 하늘을 본다
그리워 구름 타고 찾아가는 곳

절로 뚝뚝 떨어지는 설움
연못이 넘치면
비가 되어 나를 적신다

하늘 연못 참 크기도 하다
세상살이 모두 거기 있고
세상 얘기 사연들 헤엄치고 노는 곳

사랑할수록 깊어지고 넓어지고
사랑하기에 꽃들 숨 쉬고 노래하니
무지개다리 변함없이 내 맘속에 놓여있다.

김은수
한국현대시협 중앙위원,
《은점시학당》 대표,
시집 『하늘 연못』 외.

A Space Travel

Thought moving faster than light goes
to the world without disputes
to the world without wars
riding on GPT for a space travel
at the speed of 300 million kms per hour

Having passed by the moon
leaving hundreds of billion stars behind
going through 170 billion galaxies
before it realizes the bleakness of space
after traveling too far into the space

Afterwards, at full speed, it returns to home
Ah, the beautiful earth where we all live together

Kim Eun-sim
Poet, musician & travel writer. Member of Korea Music Copy Right Association. Published poetry book *Seeds* and more

우주여행

빛보다 빠른 생각이
아귀다툼 없는 세상
전쟁 없는 세상을 향해
GPT를 타고 우주여행을 떠난다
300Km의 백만배 3억Km 속도로

달을 스쳐 지나가고
수천억 개의 별들이 사라지고
1700억 개의 은하계를 통과한다
오, 적막하다
너무 멀리왔구나

다시 전속력으로 귀환한다
아, 사람들이 모여 사는 아름다운 지구

김은심
시인·음악가·여행작가.
한국음악저작권협회
회원, 시집 『씨앗』 외.

My Father's Memory

Dewdrops on yellowish green leaves and the wind
made my mother hurry in the early morning
to work in the field
Shining sunlight, grasses growing, and butterflies
led my father to the field as well

Doing their best to raise the children
they always made bright smiles
with dimples in the cheeks;
watching the wrinkles in the cheeks made by the smiles,
I wonder if they are the compensation for their hard work

Day by day
while the memory in every cell of the brain is fading away
the sunset in the west seems to remember too well
what it is supposed to do today
still, counting the dwindling numbers left

Kim Jae-won
Vice-president of Korea Sinmunye Literature Association, Awarded Esprit Literature Prize..
Published poetry book *The World in the Color of Fairy Tale* and more

아버지의 기억

이슬 머금은 연두잎과
바람은 서둘러 어머니를
들로 밀어내고
비춰진 햇살 풀 꽃나비가
아버지를 불러냈지요.

자식을 위해 최선의
삶을 살았던 해맑은
미소는 깊게 파인 보조개
주름으로 변해가는 것이
그대의 보상인가요

하루가 다르게
세포의 기억은 좁아 가는데
서산에 지는 노을은
왜 이리 잘 찾아가실까
오늘도 줄어드는 숫자를 세고 계신다

김재원
한국신문예문학회 부회장, 에스프리문학상 외, 시집 『동화빛 세상』

A Mirror

After swirling muddy water receded

Clean water comes in quietly

Looking at each other

A triangle under the water

A rectangle floating on the water

The world in a round shape inside it

Kim Jeong-hui
Member of Korea Peasant Literature Association. Coterie member of Sammool Literature Association. Published poetry book *Talking to a Whale* and more

거울

휘몰던 흙탕물 흘러가고

고요하게 앉은 맑은 물

마주 보고 있다

물아래 비친 세모

물에 뜬 네모

그 안에 둥그런 세상

김정희
한국농민문학회 회원,
샘물문학회 동인,
시집 『고래에게 말을
걸다』 외.

Let's Draw Pictures

Draw a circle in red color
Put a dot in blue color

Draw a line in yellow color
Let's draw a picture pretty and large

Draw an apple
Draw the sky in blue color

Draw a butterfly
Let's draw a picture pretty and large

Kim Jong-hwan
Former president of Munyevision Literature Association. Awarded Ha Yoo-sang Literature Prize for children's literature. Published a book *Traces of 80 years of a Life*

그림 그리자 (동요)

빨간색으론 동그라미를
파란색으론 점을 찍고요

노란색으론 노란 줄 그어
커다랗게 예쁘게 그림 그리자

빨간색으론 사과 그리고
파란색으론 하늘 그리고

노란색으론 나비 그리고
커다랗게 예쁘게 그림 그리자

김종환
《문예비전》문학회 회장 역임, 하유상문학상 동요부분 수상,
저서 『인생 80 세월의 발자취』

Power of Love

Although we stay on the earth for such a short time
we make efforts to drive darkness out of our life
while enjoying the peace in tranquility
doing our best living a life worthy of serving
as a bright light illuminating the dark path of life
giving each other consolations.
When it comes time for us to leave the earth
the light turns into the infinite force
with its wavelength transformed in the form of a circle,
penetrating into the vast universe, wandering around,
maybe, dreaming forever of another life to begin

Kim Jong-hee
Advisory committee member of International PEN, Korea Center. Advisor of The Korean Writers Association, Mapo Branch. Published poetry book *I Am Too Far Away* and more

사랑의 힘

우리가 지상에 머무는 시간이
비록 잠깐이지만,
어둠을 몰아내고 평안을 누리며
빛으로 사는 동안
서로를 비추어 위로하고
어두운 길을 밝히던 그 환한 빛은
아름다운 환(環)을 이루며 지상을 떠날 때
그 파장을 바꾸며 한없는 힘이 되어
저 광막한 우주로 스며들어
영원을 떠돌며
또 다른 탄생을 꿈꾸겠지

김종희
국제펜한국본부 자문
위원, 한국문협 마포지
부 고문, 시집 『나는
너무 멀리 있다』 외.

Mosaic of Immersive Images

With the collapse of substance
Gustav Klimt presents
Bunker des Lumières
Showing dazzling lights
Touching the inner seeds tenderly
Delightful plays with language
Rainer Maria Rilke created
As seen in hyperbolic harmony and prelude of fantasia,
After the heydays of their own history
All the artworks have come back
Like secreted sticky mucus
To be living as relics of subjects

Kim Tae-ryong
Former adjunct professor at Bucheon Univ. Awarded Korea Peasant Literature Prize. Published poetry book *Stairways of Oblivion* and more

영상 모자이크

실체의 함몰
'구스타프 크림트'의
숨겨진 찬란한 빛의 벙크가
내밀한 씨알들을
다정히 어루만지고 있었다
'릴케'가 내뱉는 감미로운
언어의 유희들
쌍곡선의 하모니 환타지의 서곡
찬란한 역사의 뒤안길에 서서
끈끈한 점액으로 토해
피사체의 유물로 살아가리라.

김태룡
부천대학 겸임교수 역임
한국농민문학상 외
시집 『망각의 계단』 외.

A Dream of New Year

With longing to be a poet in my old age
Reading books, waking up at daybreak
Speculating at night, watching the stars
I have worked hard to draw out my own words

I couldn't imagine
How much it would be embarrassing and agitating
To publish a poetry book for the readers
So I wonder if the poet is born to be

Before anybody wants to be a poet, someone said,
Develop humanity first
Keep your heart innocent and sincere
Give up any greed so as to empty your mind

Greeting the new year
I wish I could be changed a little bit
With the language of my own as a poet

Thad. T. Ghim
Steering committee member of Monthly Magazine Sinmunye. Awarded Wo;pa Literature Prize in criticism, and more. Published books, *Paying Tribute to Senior Colleague, Yoon Chi-ho* and more

새해의 꿈

늦은 나이에 시인으로 살고파
동트면 책 읽고
별 보며 사색하고
공들여 그려낸 언어들

세상에 내놓기가
이리 부끄러울 줄이야
이리 떨릴 줄이야
시인은 결국 타고 나는 것일까

누군가 말했지
먼저 인성을 키우라고
순수하고 진실하라고
욕심도 버리고 마음도 비우라고

신축 새해
내가 조금은 달라질 수 있으려나
시인의 언어를 찾을 수 있으려나

김태형
《월간신문예》운영위원, 월파문학상 평론부문 본상 외,
저서 『윤치호 선배를 기리며』 외.

Paradise of the Elderly

In the streets, subways and parks are many elderly people
looking like old trees once green and strong but changed in time
keeping their places with the bodies as dry as a bone
and the branches broken by the north wind in winter

The old people having gone through all the hardships in life
barely stand, feeling afraid of falling down by the wind
The elderly once were craving for longevity now are living
in the aged society with nobody to rely on

With the old people having no productive capacity
we see the increase of retirement homes and nursing homes only

Kim Ha-young
Board member of International PEN, Korea Center. Awarded The 2nd Youngrang Literature Prize and more. Published poetry book, *Rolling in the Wind at Barley Field*

노인 천국

거리, 지하철, 공원에 노인들이 많다
푸르른 나무도 세월 지나면 변하는 것
삭풍에 나뭇가지 부러진 채
앙상한 고목으로 지탱하고 있다

세상 풍상 겪어온 노인들
나뭇가지 바람 불면 쓰러질 듯
인간 장수 소망하던 사람들이
의지할 곳 없는 고령사회 되었다

세계는 노동력 없는 노인들이 많아
노인 타운, 요양원만 늘어간다

김하영
국제펜한국본부 이사
제24회영랑문학상 외
시집『보리밭 바람에
일렁이며』외.

Hunger

Heavy
Clump of flowers

Intoxicated
by the colors

Looking back
to see it wriggling

The road

Cut
By the teeth of a saw

With frozen dream

Here

Looking corpulent and dull
People live in bunches, eating and drinking

In the town of humanity

Kim Haeng-sook
Member of Korea Modern Poets Association. Awarded Midang Poetry Legacy Prize. Published poetry book *Forlorn Hands*

허기

무거운
꽃 덩어리

그 색깔에
취해

돌아보니
꿈틀거리는

길

톱날에
잘려나간

얼어붙은
꿈

여기

비둔함을 모른 채
먹고 마시는 족속이 모여 사는

사람의 마을

김행숙
현대시인협회 회원,
미당시맥상 수상 외,
시집 『적막한 손』 외.

A Night in Spring

At night pitch-black even without the stars shining
raindrops fall like tears of a girl

Missing the first lover I broke up with a long time ago
I try to write your name and erase it
drawing your face in the dark sky at night

During the night in spring coming as usual every year
I try to call you silently
who seems to be coming towards me with a loving heart

Thinking about the chance to see you somewhere
I close my eyes gently and slowly
hoping for meeting you even in my dream

After the rainy long night
I find plum blossoms that resembles you
bursting into bloom by the fence like popcorn flakes

Kim Hyun-sook
Member of The Korean Writers Association. Awarded Dokdo Literature Contest Prize. Published poetry book *Messages of Flowers* and more

봄밤

별 하나 없는 까만 밤하늘에
소녀의 눈물처럼 떨어지는 빗방울

오래전 헤어진 첫사랑이 그리워
썼다가 지워보는 너의 이름과
까만 밤하늘에 너의 얼굴을 그려본다

해마다 지나간 봄밤이지만
애틋한 마음으로 다가오는 너를
소리 없이 불러도 본다

어디선가 만날 것 같은 너를
꿈속에라도 만날 수 있을까
사르르 눈을 감는다

봄비 내리는 긴 밤 지새고 나면
담장 옆에 너를 닮은 매화가
팝콘처럼 터져 있다

김현숙
한국문인협회 회원,
독도문예대전 특선,
시집 『꽃의 전언』 외.

Rose of Sarajevo

The scars were filled with red resin, I was told by a tour guide,
not only to cover the traces of mortar explosions
but also to remember the tragic history of the city

Red resin,
I hadn't heard about it until then
The scars made from the explosion were filled with resin
appearing like roses, so local people called it 'Rose of Sarajevo'

'Rose of Sarajevo'
I had seen a picture of a rose stuck in the gun barrel of a tank,
the picture drawn by a boy in Sarajevo during the siege of Sarajevo,
that touched the hearts of all the people in the world

During the tour, at the picture that kept occurring to my mind
I couldn't take my eyes off from 'Rose of Sarajevo'

Kim Ho-woon
Novelist. Currently the 28th President of The Korean Writers Association. Awarded The 6th Green Literature Prize. Published many novels including *Rose of Sarajevo*

사라예보의 장미

총탄 자국을 빨간색 페인트로 메운 건물들
총탄 자국을 지우려고 그랬단다
여행자 안내소 직원이 오래 기억하기 위해
서란다

빨간 고무 페인트,
고무 페인트가 있다는 사실도 처음 알았다
빨간 고무 페인트로 메꾼 총탄 흔적
이곳 사람들은 '사라예보의 장미'라 부른다

사라예보의 장미,
언젠가 탱크 포구에 장미 한 송이를 꽂아놓은 그림,
내전으로 고립되었을 때 사라예보의 한 어린이가 그린
이 그림이 전 세계인의 가슴을 울렸다

그 그림이 떠올라, 나는
'사라예보'의 장미에서 눈을 뗄 수가 없었다.

김호운
소설가, 현)제28대
한국문인협회 이사장,
제6회 녹색문학상 수상
외, 저서 『사라예보의
장미』 외.

The Sunset

At the sunset
in the wind blowing cold
on the onset of winter passing by
I watch outside the window

Fallen leaves of ginko tree
in red hue

Blown in the wind
swirling in a circle in the air
before they disappear into nowhere

In the west of the sky
at the ridge of a mountain
time stays for a while
shedding tears of blood

Kim Hwan-saeng
Former high school principle. Awarded Literature Prize of the American branch. Published poetry book *Old Pine Tree* and more

저녁놀

찬바람 부는
다저녁
입동立冬을 보내며
창窓밖을 본다.

떨어진
붉은 단풍잎

바람에 날려
허공虛空을 맴돌다
저 멀리 사라진다.

하늘 서西쪽
산마루터기에
잠시暫時 머문 세월歲月이
피눈물을 뿌린다.

김환생
고교 교장 역임,
미주지회문학상 외,
시집 『노송老松』 외.

Family

At desolate night
the fingerprints made by the gusty wind
are left all over the window
At the places like Mt. Alps of the world
for those people suffering hard life,
eating ice flowers
mending broken stone wall trails, though,
there are places to return
Where little grass flowers are in bloom
along the winding path
from far away
or from a short distance away
coming in a pianissimo
the sounds of family member's footsteps
make the warmth hang inside of the house
for those waiting for the family

Kim Whoo-ran
President of House of Literature in Seoul. Awarded Gongcho Literature Prize and more.
Published poetry book *I Like to Visit the Island* and more

가족

거치른 밤
매운바람의 지문이
유리창에 가득하다
오늘도 세상의 알프스 산에서
얼음꽃을 먹고
무너진 돌담길 고쳐 쌓으며
힘겨웠던 사람들
그러나 돌아갈 곳이 있다
비탈길에 작은 풀꽃이
줄지어 피어있다
멀리서
가까이서
돌아올 가족의 발자국 소리가
피아니시모로 울릴 때
집안에 감도는 훈기
기다리는 사람이 있다

김후란
《문학의집서울》이사장, 제25회 공초문학상 수상 외, 시집 『그 섬에 가고 싶다』 외 다수.

Time

Only with the name
Neither in visible
Nor with sound
Nobody knows the shape

Just
Flowing endlessly
Being given fairly to everybody
In its transparent space

If you pay no attention to time
Running so fast
What it left behind is a failure

If you cherish it
Happily all together
What it left behind is a success

Nam Hyeon-u
President International Literature Association. Awarded The 2nd Ha Yoo-sang Literature Prize and more. Published poetry book *The Road Leading To Us*

시간

이름만 있을 뿐
보이지 않고
소리도 없으니
어찌 그 모습을 알 수 있으랴

다만
끝없이 흘러가며
모두에게 공평하게 주어지는
투명한 공간

소홀히 멀리하면
순간으로 흘러가서
실패를 남겨놓고

소중히 즐겁게
함께 하면
성공을 놓고 간다.

남현우
국제문단문협 회장, 제
2회 하유상문학상 외,
시집 『우리로 가는 길』

Persimmons

When I visited the old home of my mother
grand mother with her gentle smile
took me to the platform for crocks at the back yard

After removing the rice husks piled up in a crock
I could see red persimmons smiling bashfully
having the skin like the cheeks of a baby
just waking up from a deep sleep

When summer comes every year
I remember the red persimmons
grand mother used to feed me
with a spoonful of persimmon's flesh
sitting on the wooden floor
where I fell asleep with grand mother's love

Noh Sin-bae (Neung-In)
Poet, essayist, music composer. Chief buddhist monk a Hangbok temple of Geumkang meditation order in Korea Buddhism. Published poetry book *Neung-In's Talking Nonsense* and more

홍시

한여름 외갓집 가면
외할머니의 온화한 미소에 끌려
뒷마당을 돌아 장독을 연다

소복이 쌓인 왕겨를 헤치면
깊은 잠에서 깨어난
갓난아기 볼처럼
빨간 홍시가 배시시 웃고 있다

해마다 여름이 되면
뒤 칸 마루에 앉아
한 술 두 술
입맛 함께 다시며 먹여주시던
외할머니의 사랑 속에 잠든
홍시가 생각난다.

노신배
시인·수필가·작곡가,
한국불교금강선원
행복사 주지,
시집 『능인의 허튼소리』 외.

A Song of the Peasant's Wife

Still having half of lifetime to live
in the sunlight coming from the sky to the earth
I will live like grasses as a wife of a peasant, my love,
who is as generous as the shade of a mountain

In the town apricot blossoms and balloon flowers bloom
wearing loose-fitting pants, sowing the dream of my husband
I will live a life with the sunburned face in bronze

Despite long droughts, frequent floods
devastatingly dry land destroyed with cracks,
I will cultivate the fields as if raising kids with care
singing songs with craving heart for the fertile land

Putting efforts into the soils for half the lifetime left
to engrave in the land the name of the virtuous peasant
I will live a life as his companion glowing like the sunset

Roh Hee
Member of International PEN, Korea Center. Board member of Korea Christian Poets Association.
Published poetry book *A Woman Who Discards A Hundred to Gain Just One* and more

촌부의 노래

반나절은 족히 남은 생
하늘에서 땅으로 내려온 해 긴 날
산그늘 같은 내 그리운 님 아낙이 되어
풀잎 같은 촌부로 살아가리니

살구꽃 도라지꽃 피는 마을에서
헐렁한 몸뻬바지 입고 지아비 꿈 파종하는
구릿빛 얼굴로 살아가리니

오랜 가뭄과 잦은 홍수
갈라지고 무너진 피폐한 토지
어린아이 키우듯 자분자분 일구며
비옥한 땅 그리는 뜨건 노래 부르리니
흙 속에 반생을 묻는, 별을 묻는
거룩한 농부의 반려 감히 그 이름 땅에 새기고자
노을 같은 지어미로 나 이제 살아가리니

노희
국제펜한국본부, 한국 기독시협 이사,
시집 『하나를 얻기 위해 백을 버린 여자』 외.

A Repairperson of the Mind

While walking on the street absent-mindedly
suddenly thinking I am all alone
I feel the cold wind blowing in the mind

At the moment, though, I know
the world revolves around me at the center
constantly without a rest

That's why I sow a seed of flower again
in the garden of my soul
waiting for the coming spring

I love myself
always keeping the heart warm inside

Ryu In-soon
Board member of World Writers Association. Member of International PEN, Korea Center & Korea Music Copyright Association

마음 수리공

무심히 길을 걷다
문득 혼자라고 느낄 때
가슴속 찬 바람 불지만

이 순간도
세상은 나를 중심으로
쉼 없이 돌고 있음에

내 영혼 뜰 안에
꽃씨 하나 다시 심고
새봄 기다리며

내가 나를 사랑하고
내가 내 마음 데운다.

류인순
사)세계문인협회 이사,
국제PEN한국본부 회원,
(사)한국음악저작권협회
회원.

Persona

People in white clothes are passing by
on a wagon decorated with flowers, scattering seeds
In the streets they have passed with the seeds of dream
buildings awake, revealing themselves disorderly,
making the scene with penthouses looking much higher
and with peacocks spreading their fancy wings

On a building appearing chic with its modern characteristic
a red snake moves out of the view, sliding softly on its belly
Transparent Satan made by the development of civilization
looks down the parade, sneering at the people wearing
masks
running up and down the tower humans built with hard
works
Oh, Lord, You don't have any means to deal with it?
In desperate prayers made under the masks hiding audacity
not a drop of tears can be found

Maeng Sook-young
Board member of International PEN, Korea Center. Awarded Seoul City Literature Prize of The Korean Writers Association. Published poetry book *Laurel Wreath of the Sunlight* and more

페르소나

흰옷 입은 사람들 꽃차를 타고
씨를 뿌리며 지나간다
꿈의 씨앗 품은 욕망의 수레 지나간
거리엔 우후죽순처럼 드러난 건물들
기지개를 켠다
펜트하우스도 덩달아 높이
공작새는 화려한 날개를 펼친다

모던한 캐릭터의 시크한 건물
빨간 뱀 한 마리 스르르 미끄러져 나간다
문명의 발달에 변신한 투명 사탄
인간이 쌓아놓은 공든 탑 제멋대로
오르내리며 마스크의 행렬을 조롱하며
바라본다
오, 하느님 당신도 어찌할 수 없으십니까
뻔뻔함을 감춘 마스크 가면 속 울부짖는
기도엔
한 방울의 눈물이 부재다

맹숙영
국제펜한국본부 이사,
한국문협 서울시문학상
외, 시집 『햇살 월계관』
외.

Greeting the Sunlight

Coming in and out
you softly slip through fingers
tenderly tickling them when I try to grasp

You are here even before I know
listening to the stories of everything
lightly brushing against yellow petals
with rustling sounds
making us smile pleasantly

Driving into the bosom
wavering with pink colored shyness,
spring breeze, you are here

Mo Sang-cheol
Vice president of Munye Choonchoo. Awarded Sinmunye Literature Prize. Published poetry book *One Third Marginal Humming*

햇살 나들이

손가락 사이로 넘나들더니
꼭 움켜쥐면 살며시 빠져나가고
살갑게 간지럽힌다

어느덧 다가온 너
온갖 만물의 담소에 귀 기울이고
살며시 스치어가면 톡톡
노란 꽃잎 살랑살랑
반가운 미소를 짓게 하는 너

가슴을 헤치며 파고드는
분홍빛 수줍음이 너울대던
봄바람이었구나

모상철
문예춘추 부회장, 신문
예문학상 외,
시집 『3분의1
언저리의 흥얼거림』

Into the Curved Space of Time

Behind your back I let go of
swirls a strong wind;
in the sky turned around us
looks sad the pale moon at the day time

From the eyes closed
rolls down hot tears;
sitting down with legs felt drained
the tears restrained for a long time
start to fall down all at once

Ah! Time being nonchalant
Just forget about it, my friend
Our life is meant to be following time
going into the curved space of time on the road

Park Kyung-hee
Committee member of The Korean Writers Association. Editor in chief of monthly magazine
Sinmunye. Published poetry book *I Feel Hungry, Looking up into the Sky*

굽은 시간 속으로

보내는 너의 등 뒤로
세찬 바람이 휘둘고
뒤돌아선 하늘엔
창백한 낮달이 슬프다

감았던 두 눈엔
뜨거운 눈물이 흐르고
풀린 다리 주저앉으며
참고 참았던 오열이
한꺼번에 터져 나온다

아! 무심한 세월이여
잊고 가거라, 나의 친구여
시간을 따라가는 삶이여
모두가 가야 하는 굴곡의 그 길

박경희
한국현대시협 위원,
《월간신문예》 편집장,
시집 『하늘을 바라보면
배가 고프다』

Longing

In the vegetable garden
pushing off the gravels
sprouts grew, standing up

Under the warm sunlight
seeing the sun
watching the stream
they could have eatables
hidden in the manure heap

Seed leaves all have grown up
laughing and smiling
blooming yellow flowers

At the empty playground
that bees and butterflies left after having a party
thrives a sense of wistfulness only

Where a blue bird used to flutter
with the wings like tiny little hands
in good old days

Park Ki-im
Member of Korea Christian Poets Association. Awarded Wolpa Literature Prize. Published poetry book *My Love Forever*

그리움

텃밭에
자갈을 밀어내고
일어선 새싹

따스한 햇살 아래
햇님도 보고
시냇물도 보고
퇴비 속에 숨은
먹거리도 먹고

떡잎이 성큼 자라
활짝 웃더니
노랑꽃을 피웠다

벌 나비 날아와
부벼대며 놀다간 자리
아쉬움만 무성하게 자랐다

먼 옛날
파랑새 한 마리
고사리손 흔들던 시절

박기임
한국기독교시인협회
회원, 월파문학상 외,
시집 『내 사랑 영원히』

Cultivation of Relationships

For relationships
let's set up a garden
to cultivate

In the garden of mind
let's sow the seeds first
to grow our heart fluttering

Slowly nourishing the elements of love
such as consideration and concession
patiently waiting for the time
while watering the seeds

Afterwards
we see the flowers of relationships bloom
in the garden of joy

Park Gil-dong
Poet, essayist. Member of International PEN, Korea Center. Published poetry book, *A Bachelor of the Chestnut House*

인연 가꾸기

인연의
텃밭을 마련하고
가꾸어 보자

마음 밭에
제일 먼저 설레임이라는
씨앗을 심고

사랑의 태양이 되는
배려와 양보를 자양분 삼아
천천히
기다림이라는 물을 주면

마침내
환희의 텃밭에
한송이 인연의 꽃이 피어난다

박길동
시인·수필가, 국제펜한
국본부 회원,
시집 『밤나무집 도령』

Difference of Thought

As said from the olden times, "women take care of men,"
that's what I knew as truth until I saw a man
helping a drunken girlfriend wrapped up with his coat

A grandmother known to nobody
tries to find some books she is interested in
from a stack of old books thrown out in a recycling bin

I wonder
if I would be thrown out like the old books
or remain as a person with scents in people's memories

So much surprising fact I found recently is
the total amount of donation I received is exactly
the same amount of money I was embezzled

Sounding like a nonsense
but it's true and it became a turning point of my life
Changing our thoughts that's what matters

Park Du-ik
Board member of Hanmaik Writers Association. CEO of Realization of Social Justice Citizen's Solidarity. Published poetry book *Real Literature*

생각의 차이

자고로 여자가 남자를 보살피는 줄
알았는데
술에 취해 널브러진 여자 친구를
남자가 외투로 감싸고

용도 폐기하여
분리수거된 서적 더미에
갖고 싶은 책을 찾느라 분주한 할머니

나는 언제쯤
내다 버려질 존재이냐
주위에 향기로운 기억으로 남을 것인가

너무나 신기한 것이
내가 그간 받았던 기부 금액과
횡령당했던 금액이 정확히 일치하다니

황당무계한 사람 같은데
생각을 바꾸어 보니
나의 인생을 바꾼 계기가 된 듯

박두익
한맥문학가협회 이사,
사)사회정의실현시민
연대 대표,
시집 『사실문학』

Blooming Camellia Flowers

As soon as flowers bloomed they were plucked off
As soon as they opened they were forced to close
Before they turned red, they were crushed down

What would be there at the bottom of the box of Pandora
What would be left at the end of a desert-like life
Hopes would be found after all despairs are drawn out, some say,
What if the sands are still there even after they are all drawn out?

In the desert neither with milestone nor the way to return
But only with the mind being crumbled like the sands
Being broken into so many pieces
Yet craving to move forwards, crawling all the way

Despite bloody pus made on the knees
With no prospect of spring coming back again
I will crawl forwards to see
The blooming red camellia flowers at all costs

Park Mi-sum
Ph. D. in literature at Yonsei Univ. Awarded the Prize in criticism at the New years Literary Contest sponsored by Dong-A Ilbo. Member of Sinmunye Literature Association

동백 개화

피자마자 꺾어버렸다
열리자마자 닫아버렸다
붉어지기 전에 짓이겨버렸다

판도라의 상자 밑바닥엔 무엇이 있을까
사막 같은 삶의 끝엔 무엇이 남아 있을까
절망을 다 퍼내면 희망이 남는다는데
모래를 다 퍼내면 여전히 모래만 남을까

돌아갈 길도 이정표도 없는 사막에서
모래처럼 부서지는 마음아
산산조각 난 채로
기어서라도 가고 싶은 마음아

무릎에 피고름 고인다 해도
다시는 봄이 오지 않는다 해도
기어서 가겠다
붉은 동백을 기어코 보고 말겠다

박미섬
연세대학교에서 문학 박사학위 취득, 동아일보 신춘문예 평론 당선, 신문예문학회회원.

A Lotus Flower

A Life
Planted in the mud

Listening to the sounds
Of water flowing

Putting forth the bud of life
In the chaotic swamp

Living in the purified form
In the filthy world

Showing
The bliss of Heaven

Park Byung-kyu
Head of MunyeSacho at Seosan Branch. Awarded Choi Nam-sun Literature Prize and more.
Published poetry book *I Wonder if I Know Real Me*

연꽃

뻘 속에 희망이
심어진 삶

세상 물소리
귀 기울이며

어지러운 늪에
인생꽃 봉오리져

얼룩진 누리
정화로 살면서

극락세계를
공연하는 구나

박병규
문예사조 서산 지부장.
최남선 문학상 외.
시집 『나는 나를 아는가』

Tears of My Mother's Life

Living through life's ordeal
in time flying fast in a blink of an eye, I wonder,
how much my mother has been missing
her husband who left home and never returned

Going to the central front with barbed wires set up
"I gotta go. Take care of the kids"
her husband said bluntly in short
before he left home on the dusty road

He should have left a little more of love to his wife
whose burning heart was not ready yet to let go of him
Watching my mother staring at the sky with the eyes getting wet
holding a warm bowl of cooked rice wrapped up in blanket,
I realized that's the way my mother loved my father
for I saw her tears in the moonlight staying over her face

Park Byeong-rae
Former president of The Korean Writers Association at Andong Branch. Awarded Kyungbuk Women's Literature Prize. Published poetry book *Yes. It's a Miracle* and more

엄마 삶의 눈물은

질곡 없는 삶 어디 있으랴
눈 떴다 감으니 흐르는 건 세월인데
길 떠나 낯선 곳 살고 있는
그가 얼마나 그리웠을까

중부 전선 철책선이 그리 중요하던지
가마! 아이들 잘 보거라
고작 그 한마디 던져 놓고
먼지 품은 신작로 길 속으로 들어갔다

화끈거리는 가슴 진정도 안 되었는데
품속 사랑 조금 더 남겨놓고 갈 일이지
붉어 오는 눈시울에 먼 하늘 담아 들고
아랫목 구들에 묻어두었던
밥 한 그릇 안고 나오며 이게 사랑인가
달빛 머무는 순간 엄마의 눈물을 보았다

박병래
한국문협 안동지부장
엮임, 경북여성문학상,
시집 『그래 기적이야』
외.

To Andromeda

The most beautiful in the universe
Containing fabulous stars uncountable
You are the princess of Ethiopia

Radiating from too far away
You don't seem to hear the confession
Of my love I am sending you

Park Seong-jin
Poet, musician & travel writer. Member of Korea Music Copyright Association. Published poetry book *Hello, My love, My Mister*

안드로메다에게

우주에서 가장 아름다운 이여
거대한 무리를 거느린 눈부신 이여
에디오피아 공주여

너무 멀어서
내 고백이 들리지 않나요
사랑을 전할 수 없어요

박성진
시인·음악가·여행작가,
한국음악저작권협회
회원, 시집 『안녕 나의
사랑 나의 아저씨』 외.

A Silkworm Cocoon

Is a pupa or a silkworm sleeping in a cocoon
like Schrodinger's cat? Is it alive or dead if I check it out?
I like to open the cocoon to observe quantum phenomena

In the cocoon where life, love, loneliness are all overlapped
I wonder how long a silkworm would have been waiting
to write poems in silence while producing silk

For the poems embroidered with the silk of reunion, parting, longing,
all shining particles of love, my mother would have turned the spinning wheel
to reel the thread on a spool so many times, chanting in low voice

Park, Seong-cheol
Member of Korea Poets Association. Awarded Kyungbuk Literature Prize. Published poetry book *Trio in Dissonance and more*

누에고치

저 고치 안에 번데기 혹은 누에가 슈레딩거의 고양이처럼
잠자고 있을까? 확인하는 순간 살아 있을까 죽어 있을까?
누에고치를 열어 양자$_{量子}$ 현상이 있나 보고 싶다.

생명과 사랑 고독과 기다림이 중첩된 운명의 고치 속에서
누에는 명주실을 잣는 그 기나긴 시간을 얼마나 고요히
시를 쓰고 읊고 기다렸는가?

시절인연 따라 재회와 이별과 그리움의 실 오라로 수$_{繡}$를 놓은
사랑의 빛과 입자들이 여문 하얀 시, 어머니는 나직이 창$_{窓}$을
내시며 물레를 몇 바퀴나 돌려서 그 시를 다 감을 수 있었으랴.

박성철
한국시인협회 회원,
경북문학상 외,
시집 『불협화음 3중주』
외.

The Winter of Mt. Balwangsan

A mountain road full of silvery snow
being scattered all over the place
looks as beautiful as buckwheat flowers

At every tree
snowflakes are piled up like blooming flowers
with frozen frost on the branches

The traces of history accumulated
layer upon layers over 100 millions of years
look like dancing along with snowflakes in the wind

In a snowy country under the spell of magic
holding a sense of fluttering heart, happiness, and joy

The winter manifests a mysterious world
making stitches in embroidery
of fairy tales like in children's literature

Park sook-ja
Board member of The Korean Writers Association. Awarded Hwang Geum-chan Literature Prize and more. Published poetry book *Purchasing a Basket of Spring*

발왕산의 겨울

은빛으로 쏟아져 내리는 길
하얗게 뿌려진
메밀꽃처럼 아름답다

나무마다 다양한
눈꽃을 피워낸 상고대

수억 년 바람과 함께
켜켜이 쌓은 역사의 흔적들도
꽃송이와 함께 춤을 춘다

마법에 걸린 설국에서
설렘, 기쁨, 환희를 담으며

동화 속 요정들의 이야기
신비로운 세상에 펼쳐
한 땀 한 땀 수를 놓는다.

박숙자
한국문협 이사, 황금찬 문학상 외, 시집 『봄 한 바구니 사 들고』 외.

Love of Autumn

Oh, please, come here
following cosmos flowers swaying
on the path of golden field

Rubbing your face
against autumnal leaves glowing red
come to me in the shape as beautiful as you are

If you feel tired on the way
take a rest lying on red tinged leaves
of marigold booming in full

With the clouds flowing in the blue sky
ah, all over the places is the paradise
overflowing with our love

Park Young-kon
Member of The Korean Writers Association. Awarded Munyesajo Literature Prize. Published poetry book *The Wind Being with Reminiscence*

가을 사랑

임이여 오소서
황금 들녘
한들거리는 코스모스길 따라

붉게 타는 단풍잎에
얼굴 비비며
고운 모습 그대로 내게 오소서

오다가 힘들면
금잔화 뒤덮인
단풍 잎새에 누워 보세요

떠가는 구름과 파란 하늘
아~ 천지는 온통 아늑한
우리들 사랑의 천국입니다

박영곤
한국문인협회 회원,
문예사조문학상, 시집
『바람은 추억을 타고』

Love of Cosmos Flowers

When autumn comes
the memory of the first love buried in the heart grows
to bloom like cosmos flowers swaying in light pink

Without saying a word to express my mind,
just hanging around her house at the sandy field near the river,
hiding in pine forest, timidly watching her with the pounding heart or leaning on the window, singing serenades silently
I got all soaked in the dewdrops of the dawn
I miss the time when I breathed harshly
with the pounding heart scorched all in black

When autumn comes
I am out again on the path lined with cosmos flowers in light pink
going back to the time we crossed the Seomjin river by ferry
imagining the girl, my first love in the heart

Park Won-seok
Steering committee member of Asian Pacifis Writers Association & Siwon Literature Association. Currently, CEO of Park Won-ki's Seolleongtang

코스모스 연정

가을이 오면
가슴 한편 씨앗으로 묻어둔 첫사랑
연분홍 코스모스로 피어 한들거린다네

좋아한단 말 차마 못 하고 서성이던
섬진강 변 황금 모래밭 소녀의 집 앞
솔숲에 숨어 바라만 보아도 뛰는 가슴
샛별이 빛을 잃을 때까지
소녀의 창가에 기대어
새벽이슬 맺히도록 부르던 세레나데
새까맣게 타들어간 심장 할딱거리며
가쁜 숨 몰아쉬던 때 그리워

가을이 오면
나룻배 건너던 그 시절로 돌아가
연분홍 코스모스 꽃길에서
그 소녀 그려본다네

박원석
아태문인협회 운영위원,
시원문학회 회원,
현)박원기설렁탕 대표

Snow in Spring

The wind blows all over the place full of flowers
imbuing the heart with the color of petals
making it flutter like a virgin's

Ah,
how pretty it is
royal azaleas tremble with blushing faces
at the sound of the coming footsteps of you

Ah, how bashful it is
their intimate stories would be imbued
with the white color of snow coming in spring

Park Eun-sun
Member of International PEN, Korea Center. Awarded the 18th Hwang Jin-hee Literature Prize and more. Published poetry book *The Secret Only the Sea Knows*

춘설

꽃대궐에 바람 부니
꽃잎 젖어 물든 가슴
숫처녀마냥 두근대네

아~
이뻐라
홍조 띤 얼굴에 파르르 떠는 철쭉잎
그대 오시는 발자국 사그락 사그락

아~
부끄러워라
내밀한 이야기
흰 눈에 물들어버리겠네

박은선
국제펜한국본부 회원,
제18회 황진이문학상
외, 시집 『바다만 아는
비밀』

The Sound of the Coming Spring

From somewhere
comes a whispering

Passing over the frozen earth
coming through tree branches
blows the spring breeze

Expecting to see you
with the heart fluttering

I am waiting for you
in the scent of spring sweet and green

Calling for you
from the bottom of my heart
with the eyes wide open

Park Jong-hwa
President of World Environment Literature Association. Director of Psychology of Addiction Research Center. CEO of Forest Business Management Education Association.

봄이 오는 소리

어디선가
들려오는 속삭임

언 땅 찬 바람지나
나뭇가지 사이로
불어오는 봄바람

박종화
세계환경문학협회 총
재, 중독심리상담연구
소장, 숲경영교육협회
대표

설레이는 마음으로
너를 기다리며

향긋한 봄 내음과
푸른 기다림 속

가슴 깊은 곳에서
너를 부르며
눈을 뜨고 있다

Onions

A treasure hidden in the chest of soil
secretly made in the whisperings of the darkness
having the body pure and transparent
Mother earth made you looking like magnolia flowers

Peeled off the skin
your naked body cut into slices, put over a salad,
gives a taste of love rich and happy

On the frying pan sizzling hot in the oil
the transparent slices become caramelized in the heat;
meantime, I see the tears rolling out of your body
chopped into pieces by knife, making me cry, too,
for your sacrifice, putting me in nostalgia of the soil

Park jin-woo
Vice-president of Seoul Future Art Association, Awarded the 10th Esprit Literature Prize.
Board member of Seoul City's Kyuko Musical

양파

흙의 가슴에 감춰진 보석
어둠의 비밀로 빚어진 속삭임
맑고 투명한 몸은 목련을 부풀린 듯
대지는 너를 그렇게 빚었나 보다

싱싱한 네 몸을 벗긴다
샐러드에 드러난 조각난 알몸
얼마나 풍요로운 사랑과 감동인지

뜨겁게 달군 후라이팬에
잘게 썬 투명함이 기름의 열기에 변하는
모습
칼로 자를 때 자국마다 방울진
너의 눈물은 나의 눈을 울게 하는
쓰러질 때까지 흙의 향수를 전하는 희생
이다

박진우
서울미래예술협회 부
회장, 제10회 에스프리
문학상, 사)서울시립큐
코뮤지컬 이사.

Today is Still a Great Day, Anyway

Weary, hard life
A lot of stuffs to worry about
People I loved having left me
Things gnawing at my soul
With all of these causing me pains today

The blue sky, a puff of wind
Radiating sunlight, clouds and rains
Snowy evenings
Starry nights
Beautiful mountains and streams

Taking a walk at daybreak
Working hard
Planting flower seeds, taking care of trees
Having a tea together with others
Today is still a great day
Anyway

Park Chul-un
Poet, lawyer, politician Awarded Seopo Literature Prize and more. Published poetry book *A Small Lamplight and more*

오늘이 좋아 그래도

고단한 살림살이
숱한 근심 걱정
사랑하는 이들이 떠나가고
영혼마저 갉아먹는
고통의 오늘이라도

소라빛 하늘, 한줄기 바람
빛나는 햇살, 구름과 비
눈 내리는 저녁
별이 반짝이는 밤
아름다운 산천山川

새벽길을 걷고
열성껏 일하고
꽃을 심고 나무를 가꾸고
함께 따스한 차 한잔할 수 있는
오늘이 좋아
그래도

박철언
시인·변호사·정치가,
서포문학상 외, 시집
『작은 등불 하나』 외

Love Song of the Sunset

The sun setting in the west
spreads with longing its light over the horizon
embracing dead quietness forlornly

In the sky engulfing weary work of the day
joy and sorrow exist no more
but starlights only shine brightly in the void

All the whispering lights of the sunset fell asleep
and a piece of memory mixed in love and hatred disappears
in the symphony of the darkness

Park Cheol-woo
Member of The Korean Writers Association. Awarded Manri Literature Prize. Published poetry book *Song of Resurrection*

노을 연가

서산에 지는 해는
그 뉘를 그리며
적막강산 쓸쓸히 품었으랴

고단한 일과 게눈 감추듯
기쁨도 슬픔도 앗아간 빈 허공엔
별빛만이 초롱초롱 열매 맺히고

도란도란 속삭이던 광채마저 잠이 든
어둠의 교향곡에
살포시 사라지는 애증의 추억 한 조각

박철우
한국문협회원, 만리문
학대상 외, 시집『부활
의 노래』외.

Momentary, Momentary

While a drink is brimming and brimming
Solitude is brimming and brimming

While a drink is scared for being brimming and brimming
The world goes momentary and momentary

While a drink is momentary and momentary
Existence is brimming and brimming

Momentary, brimming brimming momentary momentary, scared for being brimming
momentary brimming, scared for being brimming, brimming brimming, scared for being brimming

Momentary momentary momentary momentary
Brimming brimming brimming brimming

Bae Sung-rok
Member of The Korean Writers Association & Reunion Literature Association. Published book
Knowing Dementia Makes Us Win Dementia

찰나 찰나

한 잔 찰랑 찰랑
고독 찰랑 찰랑

한 잔 찰라 찰라
세상 찰나 찰나

한 잔 찰나 찰나
존재 찰랑 찰랑

찰나 찰랑 찰랑 찰나 찰나 찰라
찰나 찰랑 찰라 찰랑 찰랑 찰라

찰나 찰나 찰나 찰나
찰랑 찰랑 찰랑 찰랑

배성록
한국문협 회원, 통일문학회 회원, 저서 『치매 알면 치매 이긴다』

Getting Myself Lower

Adorably pretty flowers
bloom on the plants of short stature

To take a detailed look at them
I should lie on my stomach
seeing them up close

Of things rare and beautiful
I should lower myself
falling flat on my face to see the merits

Baek Young-ho
Member of Hanmaik Literature Association. Awarded Korea Lyrical Literature Prize. Published poetry book *The Name Engraved in a River and more*

낮아지기

앙징맞게 이쁜 꽃은
키 작고 꽃이 작다

자세히 보기 위해
땅바닥에 엎디어
이리 보고 저리 보고,

귀하고 예쁜 건
내가 숙이고
엎어져야 그 속살 보여준다

백영호
한맥문학회원, 한국서
정문학상 외, 시집 『강
물에 새긴 이름』 외.

A Lake in Tranquility

Although the winter lake reflects the world with the clean eyes clean eyes, it keeps in the heart a handful of secrets of the muddy soil

Turning away from the world while craving for completeness, nobody can find the real beauty forever

If you listen to the whisperings of the murky water flowing
you can hear the stories of the truth in the world

Remember glittering water drops, too, are born in the soil
Pursuing the cleanness only while disregarding the soil you would never find real purity forever

Clean water and murky water flow through the different ways but finally they will get together, flowing in the same river

Respecting differences of our own and agreeing to disagree
let us grow together to become a part of the river

The river becomes a mirror to make the world more beautiful

Sa Wee-hwan
Poet, M.A, in law. Member of Korea Modern Poets Association. Member of guidance committee of Insadong Poets Association

고요한 호수

거울 호수 맑은 눈동자로 세상을
비추지만 그 심장에는 진흙 한 줌 비밀을
간직한다

완벽함을 갈망하며 세상을 외면한다면
진정한 아름다움은 영원히 찾지 못하리

흐린 물결 속삭임 귀 기울여 들어라
세상의 진실이 속삭이는 이야기가 들릴 것이다

반짝이는 물방울 흙 속에서 태어났음을 기억하라 맑음만을 갈망하며 흙을 외면한다면
진정한 순수함은 영원히 찾지 못하리

맑고 흐린 물 서로 다른 길을 흘러도
결국 하나의 강이 되어 세상을 옥죄고
흐르리라

각자의 모습을 존중하고 서로의 흐름을 받아들이며 함께 성장하는 강이 되사

그 강은 모든 것을 비추고 세상을 아름답게
만드는 거울이 될 것이다.

사위환
시인·법학석사, 현대시
협회원 회원, 인사동시
협회 지도위원.

Tinged Bean Leaves

Tinged bean leaves seasoned and fermented
are laid in a washbasin for sale on a market day
in a bundle of speckled leaves placed layer after layer
being tied around the middle with a dry straw

Reflected on the window of a shop
a woman looking like a tinged bean leaf passes by

Not quite familiar yet to her own appearance
getting old with grey hair and wrinkles
the woman ties around the waist with a dry straw
to tighten her loose belly skin

Seo Yeong-hui
Member of The Korean Writers Association. Awarded the 6th Asian Pacific Literature Prize and more. Published poetry book *Secret Codes of April* and more

단풍 콩잎

검붉은 대야 속 단풍 콩잎
잘 삭혀 오일장 한 틈에 놓였다
짙은 점들로 겹겹이 쌓인 몸
색 바랜 볏짚 허리띠 둘렀다

스치는 가게 유리창엔
단풍 콩잎 같은 여인이 지나가고

그녀, 나이 드는 게 처음이라
흰머리도 주름도 낯설기만 한데
굵어진 허리라도 조여볼까
볏짚 한 가닥 허리에 묶는다

서영희
한국문인협회 회원,
제6회 아태문학작품상
외, 시집 「사월의 암호」
외.

At the Riverside of The Seine in Paris

I walk on the riverside of the Seine
running through Paris

The river Seine
flowing with rainy tears

Coming out of my memory
the prime of my days flows in the sounds
of the rain falling along the river Seine

The river Seine flows in depth deeper
than the bottom of my heart in tears
soaking the scenery of Paris in blue

Sun Yu-mi
Poet, essayist, painter. Member of The Korean Writers Association. Published poetry book *A Town in White of the Scarf*

파리 세느강변에서

파리의 동맥인
세느강변을 걷는다

빗방울이 눈물이 되어
흐르는 세느강

추억 속에 머물고 있는
나의 봄날도 빗소리와 함께
세느강을 따라 흐르고

내 눈물의 뿌리보다
더 깊은 세느강이
파리 풍경을 푸르게 적시고 있다

선유미
시인·수필가·화가, 한국문협 회원, 시집 『스카프 속 하얀 마을』 외.

Arirang of Korea

Korea is the mountains you should climb over, singing Arirang,
The same song we sing with different titles in different regions,
The folk song is kept in people's heart through movies and stories

Either in the streets of Seoul or in the hills at Jeongsun, anywhere
The song kept in our heart can be heard, Arirang, Arirang, Arariyo,
The song of hometown for all of us without designating a particular region,
Whenever we go over a hill, a new narrative begins to start

With the numerous footprints connected with a single song Arirang
a new narrative is inscribed at each step while going over a hill
There are so many hills of life all over the Korean peninsular
where we can hear Arirang, the folk song of Korea filling the air

Sung Ki-hwan
Poet. M.A. in media. Vice-president of Insadong Poets Association. Awarded Tammi Literature Prize. Board member of Korea Sinmunye Literature Association

대한의 아리랑

한국은 산이 많아 아리랑 노래 부르며 넘는 산
도시마다 산골짜기마다 이름 달라도 노래는 같아
민요는 영화로 이야기로 사람들 가슴에 살아
있네

서울의 거리든, 정선의 고개든, 어디서든 들려
오는
'아리랑, 아리랑, 아라리요' 가슴에 품은 노래
정한 곳 없어,
우리 모두 고향의 그리운 노래
고개를 넘을 때마다, 새로운 이야기 시작되네

아리랑 하나로 이어진, 무수한 발자국들 속에서
걸음걸음마다 이야기가 새겨지는 고개 넘으며
한반도 곳곳에 울려 퍼지는 삶의 고갯길
온 누리에 울려 퍼지는 대한의 노래 아리랑

성기환
미디어 석사, 인사동시
인협회 부회장, 탐미문
학상 수상. 한국신문예
문학회 이사. v

Being in Disagreement

Two different thoughts
Each one with its own idea
A flower
in yellow, in pink
or in red,
all see it from a different perspective
Each one with its own idea
That's what makes the world a noisy place
or a beautiful one

Sohn Young-ran
Pastor in charge of Real Love& Hope Church. Member of The Korean Writers Association. Board member of Asian Pacific Writers Association

엇갈림

둘이 생각이 달라요
각기 다 생각이 달라요
노란꽃을 보아도
핑크빛 꽃을 보아도
빨간색 장미를 보아도
왜 생각이 천차만별인가
각기 다 생각이 달라요
그래서 세상은 시끄럽기도 하고
아름답기도 해요

손영란
참사랑소망교회 담임목사, 한국문인협회 회원, 아태문인협회 이사.

A Drinking Toast in a Loud Voice

Raising a shot glass at a company dinning
people like to make a drinking toast calling for unity

Folks, if I say "baewooja"
until the time just before death,
please say all together "baewooja," OK?

"Baewooja until the time just before death!!"
"Baewooja!!!"

Wow,
Clap, clap, clap

Son Jae-soo
Born in Andong, Kyungbuk. Member of The Korean Writers Association. Published poetry book *Dandelion's Dream* and more

외치는 소리

회식 자리에서 술잔을 들고
단합을 외치는 말소리

여러분 제가 임종 직전까지
'배우자!'* 하거든
여러분은 '배우자' 해주세요.

"임종 직전까지 배우자!!"
"배우자!!!"

와~ 우~
짝짝짝.

손재수
경북 안동 출생, 한국
문인협회 회원, 시집
『민들레의 꿈』 외.

In Front of Walyong Plum Tree with Dark Red Flowers

In front of Ahn Jung-geun Memorial Museum at Mt. Namsan in Seoul
stands a red plum tree so precious to be called Walyong plum tree*
with flowers blooming in full of fragrance in spring still cold

On March, 26th, the 113th memorial day of patriot Ahn who
sacrificed himself for the country, I walked up the fortress trail in
Mt. Namsan and stand in front of the tree

Watching the plum tree, I wonder,
if those dark red flowers are blooming
out of Ahn's sacrificing blood bled for the country

I hear the voice of Ahn from the flowers being shaken in the wind,
"If the sounds of Independence of Korea reaches me in the heaven,
I will dance shouting hooray, as I should"**
While watching the flowers with respect for patriot Ahn Jung-geun
I ask myself if he is still dancing and shouting at this moment

* Walyong plum tree: The association for commemoration of patriot Ahn Jung-geun planted a young plum tree on May 26, 1999, in order to make it succeed to the mother tree that had been deprived by the Japanese during Japanese invasion of Korea in the 16th century

** This quote is from Ahn Jung-geun's last will written in prison

Song Nak-hyun
Member of International PEN, Korea Center. Awarded The 28th Sunsoo Literature Prize. Published poetry book *River Water Writes History, Too*

와룡매臥龍梅 검붉은 꽃잎 앞에서

서울의 남산 안중근 의사 기념관 앞에
귀하디귀한 홍매화 한 그루, 이름하여
와룡매*
아직도 쌀쌀한 봄 날씨에 활짝
피어 짙은 향기를 뿜어내고 있다

의사께서 순국하신 지 113년째 되는
오늘,
2023년 3월 26일
나는 남산 성곽길을 올라 그 매화
검붉은 꽃잎 앞에 서 있다

장대한 목숨, 순국의 피가 용솟음쳐서
검붉게 검붉게 매梅꽃으로 피웠을까

바람에 흔들려 이리저리 손짓하니
"대한독립의 소리가 천국에 들려오면
나는 마땅히 춤추며 만세를 부를 것이다"**
지금 이 시각, 만세를 부르며 춤추고 계시는 것일까…
추모의 마음 가득 담아 꽃잎을 바라보고 있다

송낙현
국제펜한국본부 회원,
제28회 순수문학상 대
상, 시집 『강물도 역사
를 쓴다』 외.

* 임진왜란 때 창덕궁에 있던 나무를 일본으로 가져간 모목#木의 후계목
으로 1999년 3월 26일 '안중근의사 숭모회'에서 이곳에 심었다.
** 안중근 의사의 유언 중에서

The Dream of Magnolia

The wind blows

The spring coming this year again
lets people enjoy the time
staring at magnolia flowers

The spring going away again
lets people lament for the time
staring at magnolia flowers falling

Under the magnolia tree
having lost all the flowers
spreads a shade of loneliness only

Meantime,
paying the least attention to the fallen flowers
if they are magnolia's or not,
today, people go on their own way

Again, the dream of magnolia
indicates the beginning of longing one more time

Song Deok-young
Poet, novelist. President of Namyangjoo Poets Association. Awarded Chairman's Prize of Kyunggido Provincial Assembly. Published poetry book *The Reeds in My Mind* and more

목련의 꿈

바람이 분다

봄이 왔다는 것은
저만치 목련꽃 피는 것을
바라보는 것

봄이 간다는 것은
분분한 목련꽃의 낙화를
바라보는 것

꽃을 잃어버린
목련나무 아래
고독한 그늘이 진다

사람들은
그가 목련이었음을
아는지, 모르는지
오늘도 제 갈 길을 간다

다시, 목련의 꿈은
그리움의 시작이다

송덕영
시인·소설가, 남양주시
협 회장, 경기도의회의
장상 외, 시집 『내 마음
의 갈대』 외.

White Clouds

As if with no sufferings whatsoever
but all connected in harmony
the white clouds flow again in the sky
like the ocean waves rolling

In the space vast and endless
wandering like a shadow
embracing everything delightful or sad
the white clouds flow in the wind;
nobody knows why without going through the life

Looking clear or even transparent
flowing without a destination
into the ocean of white clouds I fall
feeling so much enthralled even before I notice

Let's not feel sad about having no hometown
My hometown is right there
where my lonely footsteps stay

Song Mi-soon
Member of The Korean Writers Association. Awarded the Prize for Travel Poems. Published book *The Sun Rises*

흰 구름

온갖 고뇌 잊은 듯
나직한 하모니의 연결
흰 구름은 다시 파도처럼
일렁이며 흘러간다

무변광대 먼 공간 위
방랑의 그림자로
기쁨과 슬픔 아우르는 삶
겪어보지 못한 사람은 알지 못한다
왜 저리 흘러가는지

맑은 듯 투명한 듯
정처 없이 흐르는
어느새 나는 빠져든다
흰 구름 바다로

고향이 없다고 서러워 말자
외로운 발길 머무는 곳
그곳이 바로 내 고향이니.

송미순
한국문인협회 회원, 기행시 부문 대상, 저서
『태양은 솟는다』

A Flower Vase

A pale flower of calla lily
withers in the shade of clothes

My mind is a flower vase for you
sinking with dried flower fragrances all mixed up

Imagining a breathtaking emotion that could be felt
at the stalk of the flower like the back of the neck

The flower vase can't sleep, feeling the heart fluttering
with a hope to soak you in water tomorrow

Song Tae-han
Board member of International PEN, Korea Center. Awarded Yeonam Literature & Arts Prize.
Published poetry book *Putting the Puzzle Together*

꽃병

해쓱한 카라 꽃송이
옷섶 그늘에서 시드네

내 가슴은 그대의 꽃병
마른 향기 엉기어 가라앉는데

꽃대처럼 숨찬 감동 한 줄기
목덜미까지 어여 차오르게

그대 흠뻑 적셔 줄 설렘으로 이 밤,
꽃병은 홀로 잠 못 이루네

송태한
국제펜한국본부 이사,
연암문학예술상 대상,
시집 『퍼즐 맞추기』 외.

Spring Breeze

Although it survived the winter
it's hard for a tree alone
to draw up water into the branches

Spring breeze swaying tree branches
to help drawing water upwards
also makes buds sprout on the branches

As I always played prank
on the girls I liked
when I was little

Spring breeze makes
a gesture of dear love

Shin Gap-sik
Graduated from graduate school of Chonnam National Univ. Published poetry book *Feeling Shy of the Moonlight*

봄바람

겨울 지난 나무
혼자서는
가지 끝물 올리기 힘들다지

나뭇가지 흔들어
물 올리기 도와주는 봄바람
그 바람에 새싹을 틔운다지

나 어렸을 적
좋아하는
여자애 늘상 괴롭혔듯이

봄바람은
지극한 사랑의 몸짓.

신갑식
전남대 대학원 졸업,
중등교장 역임, 시집
『달빛도 부끄러워』 외

Grass Flowers

Embracing cold dewdrops
beautiful grass flowers bloom
In this wide world, it is good for you
even if we don't know your names

Being born in the blessings of the heaven,
yet struggling in a thorny path of life
suffering from stormy weather and all those troubles,
you still invite bees and butterflies
It is good enough to call you
either the flowers of the sun or the flowers of the stars

For you have been teaching me
your truth
always blooming in silence

Shin Young-ok
Poet, writer of children's literature. Member of International PEN, Korea Center. Published poetry book *Going My Way on the Road*

들꽃

찬 이슬 받아 안고
곱게 피어나는 풀꽃
이 너른 세상에
이름을 몰라도 좋으리

하늘 은총으로 피어났으니
가시밭길
비바람에 휘날려도
벌 나비 맞아주는 깊은 속내
해님꽃이라 불러도 좋으리
별꽃이라 불러도 좋으리

나를 가르치는 건
언제나 말없이 피어나는
너의 진실 그 때문이지

신영옥
시인·아동문학가·작사가, 국제펜한국본부 회원, 시집 『길 위에서 길을 가다』 외.

Starwort Flowers

The stars dwelling in the sky came down
To the low place in the forest

Looking at the open sky of the daytime
I realized they were down here

Sitting modestly in a grass thicket
Making gesture of hope burning like a flame

Tonight, though,
Starwort flowers are back
In the night sky
Being the stars shinning bright again

Shin Wi-sik
Senior vice-president of The Korean Writers Association, Paju branch. Awarded Tammi Literature Prize. Published poetry book *Song of Grass, the Beginning* and more

별꽃

밤하늘에 살던 별
숲속 낮은 곳으로 내려왔네

텅 빈 낮 하늘
그댈 보고 알았네

함초롬 풀숲에 앉아
온몸 사르던 소망의 몸짓

오늘은
밤하늘에서
별이 되어 반짝이네

신위식
한국문협파주지부 수석부회장, 탐미문학상 외, 시집 『시작, 풀꽃의 노래』

The Sea at Splendid Dawn

Waiting for the sun rising up at daybreak in summer
in the ships looking like black dots moving in the first light
fishermen cast fishing nets, catching their dreams
Life force felt from thrashing and fluttering fishes in the net
along with fishermen's strong will felt in every sinew strained
make a part of life complete with joy at the moment
when the sun rises up glaring over the horizon
At the peak of dawn, I wonder
how many people prepare the meals with fish being caught
with the eyes still fresh and glittering like the sunlight
With the hopes ripened well
filling themselves passionately with the life force of the sun
the fishermen make hopes like the first light of the dawn
Making hopes, sharing love,
all these start from the sea at splendid dawn

Sin Hye-kyung
Member of The Korean Writers Association. Awarded Im Hwa Literature Prize. Published poetry book *Small Me in a Drawer*

새벽 바다

여름의 새벽 해돋이를 기다린다.
여명 속을 오가는 검은 점같은 배들이
부산히 그물을 던지며 희망을 건져 올린다.
살아 튀어 오르는 물고기들의 생명력
팽팽한 힘줄이 당겨지면서
삶의 일부가 완성되어지는 환희의 순간들
붉은 태양이 고개를 내밀기 시작한다.
새벽의 절정
어부들의 고기잡이로 몇 명의 식탁을 생선으로 채울까
타오르는 태양만큼 초롱초롱한 생선의 두 눈
잘 구워진 희망
희망을 먹고 생명력을 먹고 타오르는 태양의 정열을 먹고
새벽같은 희망을 만들 사람들
희망을 만들고 사랑을 나누고
이 모든 것들이 시작되는 황홀한 새벽 바다

신혜경
한국문협 회원, 임화문학상 작가상, 시집 『서랍 속의 작은 나』 외

A Porcelain Jar

Sitting still
Living a life
Of endless praying

Saying
No words
Neither hot nor cold

Always feeling full
Even with the stomach emptied
A jar for treasure remains aloof

Ahn Kwang-suck
Poet, essayist. Vice-president of Korea Modern Poets Association. Awarded Literature & Media Literary Prize. Published poetry book *Counting the Stars* and more

항아리

고요히 앉아
한없이
기도하는 삶

덥다
춥다
한마디도 없이

비워도
늘 배부른
초연한 보물단지

안광석
시인·수필가, 현대시협
부이사장, 문학미디어
문학상 외, 시집『별을
헤다』외.

Watercolor Painting in My mind

In the drawing paper of my mind
the sky is high and in azure
the sea is deep and in indigo

In the night sky
the stars as big as a fist
shine with bright flashes of light

In the drawing book of your mind
the sky is in blue
the sea is in deep-blue
the starlight is bright and clear like a crystal

At every night and dawn
a watercolor painting is being drawn

Ahn Yun-ja
Poet, essayist. Welfare committee member of The Korean Writers Association. Awarded the Prize ay Pyunghwa newspaper literature Contest. Published poetry books and the collections of essays

내 마음속 수채화

내 마음속 흰 도화지에는
하늘이 높고 파랗고
바다는 깊고 푸르고

어두운 밤하늘엔
주먹만 한 별들이
초롱초롱 빛나고 있습니다

네 마음속 화첩에는
하늘은 푸르게
바다는 새파랗게
별빛은 수정처럼 영롱히

밤마다 새벽마다
그림을 그립니다

안윤자
시인·수필가, 한국문협
복지위원, 평화신문공
모 대상, 시집·수필집
다수.

In an Elevator

There is a wall between us,
the wall we can see only in the mind
The imprisoned puppets of time standing by the buttons
suffer autism in the closed space
failing to keep the eyes steady
looking up at the ceiling once
dropping the eyes down to the floor again
staring vacantly, losing focus
standing with the neighbors
awkwardly reading the numbers on the buttons
until we hear the door open and see people get out
disappearing as if they were deleted

An Jae-chan
Editorial committee member of The Korean Writers Association. Awarded Cho Yeon-hyun Literature Prize. Published poetry book *Flirtatious Season* and more

승강기

우리 사이에 담이 있다
마음으로만 볼 수 있는 담
단추가 가두어 버린 시간의 꼭두각시
눈길조차 한 곳에 머물지 못하는
자폐 공간 속에서
천정 한번 올려다보고
바닥 한번 내려다보고
멀뚱거리는 경계 사이로 초침이 지나간다
넘어지면 손 닿을 이웃,
열없이 난수표만 읽다가
총총 사라지는 비정한 길
삐- 소리에 눈길마저 삭제된

안재찬
한국문협 편집위원.
조연현문학상 외. 시집
『바람난 계절』 외.

A Consequence of Being Lazy

At the rooftop when summer rainy season is over
chives that were growing with dense tufts of long leaves
have overgrown taller and sturdier over the past few days

Sometimes on a rainy day, my wife used to ask me
to come home earlier than usual with a bottle of rice wine
for seafood and chive pancake she would make for me

Having a drink with the pancake made with squid, clam meat, chives
is the best match for an evening, especially when it rains;
for today, however, I missed the chance to enjoy it for my laziness

Well, I would wait for chives coming back all in green next year

An Jong-man
Poet, essayist. President of Senior Well-being Forum. Awarded the Citation of Seoul Mayor. Published the collection of essays *Well Living, Well Aging, and Well Dying* and more

게으름의 산물

여름 장마 끝에 옥상에 올라보니
며칠 전까지 잎이 무성하던 부추가
대궁이 생기고 봉우리가 맺힌다

비 오는 날이면 가끔 일찍 들어오세요
해물부추전 해 놓을 테니
막걸리 한 병 가져오란다

풋내와 오징어 조개조합에 반주는
빗소리와 환상의 궁합이던 것을
게으름 피우다 각별한 식도락이 사라졌다

내년에 다시 푸르름 안고 오겠지.

안종만
시인·수필가, 시니어웰빙포럼 회장, 서울시장 표창장, 수필집『잘 살고 잘 늙고 잘 죽기』외.

In the Fog

The sky is always there

Being open in silence

Whether it's covered with the clouds

Or obscured with the snow and the rain

The open sky is there

Making a clean smile

Even now in thick fog

It's smiling over the peak of a mountain

Ahn Hye-cho
External cooperation committee member of The Korean Writers Association. Awarded Literature Prize of International PEN, Korea Center. Published poetry book, *In the Things Surviving* and more

안개 속에서

하늘은 늘 거기에 있네

소리없이 열려 있네

구름 떼에 뒤덮이고

눈비에 가리워도

늘 거기에 열려

마알갛게 웃고 있네

지금은 안개 자욱한

저 산봉우리 너머로

안혜초
한국문인협회 대외협력위원, 국제펜한국본부 PEN문학상 외, 시집 『살아있는 것들에는』 외.

Adobe-walled Cottage

Hey, stray cats wandering around a walk trail,
have you noticed the adobe-walled cottage
near the embankment
and the trembling candle light coming out of the place?

On the way you were passing by the place
have you ever bidden a greeting
to old man and woman who live in the cottage?

Despite the shabby appearance of the cottage
there is a spot in the room
warm and comfortable like mother's love

Frostwork forms on the adobe wall like in a painting,
And the sounds of flute made by paper weather strips
I can hear them coming from the palace of my youth
Living in a meager life of ours, though,
I wish our life to glow like blooming grass flowers

Yang Sang-gun
Adjunct professor at Dongnam Public Health College. Awarded the Prize of Yeogang Literature Association. Published poetry book *Between One and Another*

토담집

둘레길 길고양이야
뚝방길가 토담집을 보았느냐
새어 나온 간드레 불꽃이
떨고 있는 것을

그 집 앞을 지나는 길에
할배와 할매께
인사라도 드렸느냐

보기에 초라해도
어머니 사랑 같은
따끈따끈한 아랫목이 있다

토담벽에 벽화처럼 서리꽃 피었다
문풍지 사잇길로 울어대는 피리소리
어린시절 나의 아방궁
메마른 우리네 삶
풀꽃처럼 피어나리

양상군
동남보건대학교 외래
교수, 여강문학회문학
상, 시집 『하나와 하나
사이』 외.

Spring Comes like an Incoming Tide

Spring doesn't come
in a rush
It keeps coming slowly, though,
like an incoming tide

Making sandy beach in thirst
not to be choked on water
waves flow in steadily and slowly
moistening the thirsty throat of the beach

People don't have to feel embarrassed
of being dull in noticing
the spring is already in full swing
for spring always comes like an incoming tide
permeating the air around us

Yang Chang-sik
Former president Jeju International Univ & dean of graduate school. Published poetry book
The Wind Brings the Taste of Jeju Island

봄은 밀물처럼 온다

오는 봄은
한걸음에 달려오지 않는다
밀물처럼 슬금슬금
스미어온다

갈증 난 모래사장
사레들지 않게
한 모금 한 모금
목 축여주는 파도

눈치가 늦어서
어느새 봄인가 하는 사람들
부끄러워할 연유가 없다
봄은 밀물처럼
그리 스며오는 것이다

양창식
제주국제대학교총장·
대학원장 역임, 시집
『제주도는 바람이 간이
다』 외.

Feeling Tranquility

As the night gets deeper and deeper
thousands of the stars sink in the lake
At the mountain temple with no wind blowing
a flowing stream makes sound so clear

With magnolia flowers swaying softly
I feel like my eyes are closing
Ah, the bashful flesh of the moonlight
is so dazzling for my eyes

Eum Chang-sup
Professor emeritus at Kwangdong Univ. President of Kim Dong-myung Literature Association.
Published a collection of criticism *Semantic Network of Deviation fro a Routine and Differentiation*

아, 고요다

밤은 깊어 삼경三更인데
수천의 별 호수에 잠기고
바람 끊긴 산사山寺의
여울 소리 맑기도 해라.

하늘하늘 백목련 꽃잎에
사르르 감기우는 두 눈,
아흐, 월광月光의 수줍은 속살
마냥 고와 눈부셔라.

엄창섭
관동대학교 명예교수,
김동명문학회 회장,
평론집 『일상의 일탈과
차별성의 의미망』 외.

Windflowers Blooming in Byunsan

Pretty windflowers grow sticking out among the gravels covered with snow

Wavering in the wind as if fluttering the wings of angels with bright smiles

For those windflowers growing up being fed with snowflakes, hiding their beauty in shy, bright smiling petals, the stars embroider the night sky with praising song

Having been envious of the rock on the mountain ridge where windflowers growing up, the chilly crescent moon now sheds friendly lights on the rock

Windflower crouching in the cold shade with a snow hat. Please, don't feel loneliness. You would have the whirlwind staying for a company.

The spring waiting to come sooner with tears in the eyes makes a gesture with haze rising over a forest with hepaticas awakening from the cold

---

Yeo Woon
Member of The Korean Writers Association. Awarded Tthe Best Prize in contribution in literature from Kyungbuk Newspapwe. Published poetry book *Painting of Heavenly Horse*

변산 아씨 바람꽃

눈이 덮인 돌멩이 틈 사이로 빼긋이
내민 것이 앙증맞게 고와라

순백의 천사 날개 저어 하얀 미소를
폴폴 풍기며 바람에 한들거린다

끼니 밥은 눈송이 먹고 자라 부채잎
춤추듯 화려함도 숨긴 채 방실 웃음
꽃잎 속에 수줍음을 간직하니 별들까지
수를 놓아 노래하네

골짜기 등선 갈잎바위 품 안에 있어
질투하던 새초롬한 초승달도 맵시 사랑
몸빼바지로 감싸주듯 비추어 준다

추운 그늘에서 웅크린 눈 모자 쓴
바람꽃이여 외로워 하지마라 변산아씨야
지나가는 휘리바람 동무가 머물러 주지
않니

눈물지어 저만치 기다리는 봄은 노루귀
달린 얼음숲 들로 동그랗게 아지랑이
가물거리며 손짓하네

여 운
한국문인협회 회원,
경북일보 기고문 최우
수상, 시집 『천마도』

Kimchi Song

Noodle soup with radish kimchi, sweet potato with radish water kimchi Kimchi made with diced radish, leaf mustard, whole radish, or cucumber
A mouthful of cooked rice and a piece of cabbage kimchi put over it. Making the healthiest meal unnecessary of any dish made in meat. It's best food making the muscle strong, causing no indigestion. Having kimchi all year round makes us no need for other side dish

Green onion kimchi is good for boosting energy to people exhausted. White kimchi without red pepper, water kimchi with water parsley
Improving immunity, keeping the body thin, lowering blood pressure, cleaning blood vessel, helping the liver function better
Kimchi is the best source for us to take in lactobacillus
The best choice to have a good metabolism preventing adult diseases

Protecting us from artery hardening, cancer cells, skin aging
Kimchi is the dish getting two thumbs up in the sumptuous feast. Representing Korean food containing our soul and spirit all together
People around the world are in love with the taste of Korean kimchi. People around the world are in love with the taste of Korean kimchi

Oh Yeon-bok
Poet, song writer, columnist. Member of THe Korean Writers Association. Board member of Korea Modern Poets Association

김치송

국수 가락에 열무김치 고구마엔 동치미
깍두기와 갓김치 총각김치 오이소박이
김장김치 쭉 찢어 흰밥 위에 척 걸치면
고기반찬 부러우랴 보약 밥상 따로 없네
근육은 불끈불끈 소화력도 금상첨화
사시사철 김치 밥상 열 반찬도 안 부럽네

파김치 된 사람은 파김치로 위로하고
시원 청량한 백김치 나박나박 나박김치
면역력 높이고 뱃살 고혈압 가뿐해
혈관을 청소하고 간 기능도 올려준다네
살살살 잡아주는 유산균의 보물창고
신진대사 키워서 성인병 예방 최고라네

(후렴)동맥경화 암세포 피부 노화
막아주는 반찬 중 으뜸이요
진수성찬 첫째 손가락 겨레의 얼로
버무리고 혼으로 담아내는
자랑스런 한국의 맛 지구촌이 찬미하네
자랑스런 한국의 맛 지구촌이 잔미하네

오연복
시인·작사가·칼럼니스트, 한국문인협회 회원, 한국현대시협 이사.

Bibimbap*

At the moment I put the spoon in the boiled rice
I become seasoned greens in the bowl

Having a rigid but bland life
Incapable of blending with others

I crave for being crushed and mixed
Turning to be imbued in red

Well mixed with joy, anger, sorrow and pleasure
To appease somebody's hunger of the mind
I like to be a spoonful of spicy Bibimbap

*the boiled rice with assorted vegetable mixtures

Woo Young-sook
Ph.D. in literature majoring in social welfare at Hyup Sung Graduate School. Vice-president of Insadong Poets Association. Member of Asian Pacific Writers Association

비빔밥

나물밥에 숟가락을 얹는 순간
나물이 된다

뻣뻣하고 밍밍한
섞이지 못하던 삶

으깨어지고 버무려져
붉게 물들고 싶다

희로애락 비벼져
누군가 마음의 공복에 허기 달래는
한 입 매콤한 밥이 되고 싶다.

우영숙
협성대학원 사회복지학 문학박사, 인사동시인협회 부회장, 아태문인협회 회원.

Dewdrops

Coming to grass blades when the darkness fades away
with bright, untainted face glowing with dreams
dewdrops looking like bright tear drops
draw a circle, rolling on taro leaves

Freeloading at grass stems and leaves
like living in a room cold and empty for free
dying with the body getting thin gradually
dewdrops, though, are still dreaming in deep flesh

Becoming one with the sunlight,
although perishing whenever the wind blows,
the mind gets matured as much as it learns from nature;
the nature smiling at me is always for my life

Living with pure passion
being shaken briefly when the morning comes
I lie down on the grass field
getting out of the burden of life

Yoo Gyeong-ja
Member of The Korean Writers Association. Awarded the Citation from Korea National Artistic Federation, Kyunggi Branch. Published poetry book *If I Stand by the River*

이슬

어둠이 새는 동안 풀잎에서 만나
꿈이 크는 해맑은 얼굴
방울방울 토란잎 위로 구르며
동그라미 그리는 영롱한 눈물

줄기와 풀잎에 더부살이
찬 공기 스민 방에 기대어
점점 몸이 말라 죽어가면서
살 속 깊이 꿈꾸고,

햇살과 한 몸이 되어
바람이 불 때마다 소멸하지만
그만큼 성숙해지는 마음
자연의 미소는 나의 삶

순수한 열정으로 살다
아침이 오면은 짧게 흔들리며
삶의 무게 벗어나
풀밭에 눕는다

유경자
한국문인협회 회원, 한국예총경기도연합회 표창장, 시집『그 강가에 서면』

A Flower

Climbing up the hill in the wind
feeling tired and hungry
turning at the edge of a cliff
on a single path

Of a mountain
where dusty travelers gathered and scattered

I find myself being born again
as a totally different me
as if blooming at a place far away
somewhere beyond the world

Yoo Dong-ae
Former president of The Korean Writers Association at Gurye Branch. Member of Korea Women Writers Association. Published poetry book *Flowers blooming inside Me* and more

꽃

바람 부는 언덕
허기허기 올라
벼랑 끝
외줄기로 돌아

길손처럼 만나서 흩어지는
먼지 이는 대지에

이 세상 너머
어느 먼 곳에서처럼
전혀 다른 나로
태어나고 있었다

유동애
한국문인협회구례지회장 역임. 한국여성문학인 회원, 시집 『내 안에 피는 꽃으로』 외.

The Sounds of the Autumn Coming

An arbor behind the house under the hazy moonlight
looks like the one in a paradise of silent tranquility
for all the creatures living in the garden

Small and tall trees within the garden fence
stand like soldiers guarding the arbor;
pumpkin flowers bloom under the moonlight
as if tempting with yellow smiles

Shaking the quietude, insects cry out
buzzing and chirping, buzzing and chirping
letting each other know who they are
when the temperature of the wind changes
following the natural law

Yu Sook-hee
Board member of Insadong Poets Association. Awarded The 11th Wolpa Literature Prize.
Published poetry book *The Seeds Dreaming of Freedom*

가을이 오는 소리

어스름 달빛 아래
집 뒤 정자는 고요한 침묵 속에
뜰에 사는 생명들의 궁전 같네

울타리 안 크고 작은 나무들
병정처럼 서 있고 그 사이로
비치는 달빛 아래 호박꽃
유혹하듯 노랗게 웃고 있네

정적을 흔드는 벌레 우는 소리
찌르르 찌르르 귀뚤귀뚤
서로 존재감을 알리고
자연의 섭리에 순응하며
바람의 온도도 변해 가네

유숙희
인사동시인협회 이사,
제11회 월파문학상 수
상, 시집 『자유를 꿈꾸
는 씨앗』

Picking Up a Life

Near the entrance of an apartment
a withered and sick flower of moth orchid
was thrown away, looking shabby and untidy

After several days the flower would be losing its life
and being dumped away like a trash
even though it is a still breathing

Being unable to pass it by cold-heartedly
I took the flower home and treated with care for 10 days
until it revived and breathed warm again

Now, wondering how beautiful she would be looking
with colors and shapes on the face
I am looking forward to seeing her smile
with the mind so much excited day after day

Yu Jung-kwan
President of Korea Sinmunye Literature Association. Awarded Sinmunye Literature Prize in 2022. Published poetry book *Like the Wind, Like the Water*.

생명을 줍다

아파트 입구 언저리에
늙고 병든 꽃이 버려졌다
으깨어진 호접란 가녀스럽다

며칠 지나면 숨을 거두고
쓰레기로 치워야 할 생명
아직은 숨 거두지 않은 목숨

도무지 그냥 지나칠 수 없어
데려다가 10여 일 정성 들이니
따뜻한 숨 내뱉는다

어떤 색깔 어떤 모습으로
세상에 얼굴을 보여줄지
하루하루 설레는 마음으로
그녀의 웃는 모습 기다린다.

유중관
2022년도 신문예문학상 대상, 시집『바람같이 물같이』외.
현)한국신문예문학회 회장.

A Small Spring

Even with a touch of breath
Chortles
Tranquility

Yoo Chang-geun
Poet, literary critic. Professor emeritus at the department of creative literary writing of Myungji Univ. Awarded Cho Yeon-hyun Literature Prize. Published more than 50 poetry books and criticisms.

옹달샘

입김만 닿아도
자지러지는
고요

유창근
시인·문학평론가, 명지
대학교 문예창작학과
명예교수, 조연현문학
상 외. 시집 평론집
50여 권.

The Center of My Life

I draw a concentric circle around Him
He is always at the center of the circle
bringing the flowers into blossom

I realized it when I felt the stars shining inside me

Going ups and downs
He is the equilibrium weight for a balancing point
and I rely on Him, following the way obediently

Making me sit up all night
walk on the road in loneliness
feel shaken all day long yesterday
He is at the center of my life

Yoo Hyeong
President of Asian Pacific Writers Association. Awarded Environmental Literature Prize. Published poetry book *Inside the Wall of Autumn* and more

중심

그를 두고 동심원을 그린다
언제나 중심은 그에게 있다
꽃을 곱게 피우게 하는 것도

속별이 내릴 때 알아차렸다

내려갈 땐 올라가고 올라갈 땐 내려가서
잔잔히 중심을 맞춰주는 평형추
그에게 매달려 고분고분 따라가고 있다

온밤을 지새우게 한 것도
쓸쓸하게 길을 걷게 한 것도
어제 종일을 흔들렸던 것도
중심에는 그가 있다

유 형
아태문인협회 이사장,
환경문학 대상, 시집
『가을 담장 안』 외.

Canna Seeking a Solution

Feeling quite fond of your fragrance
Canna fell for you
In your eyes
Canna was found smiling in happiness
feeling like she was winning the world
for you were also happily laughing and smiling
While being together for so many hours and days
your soft touch makes her heart flutter
comforting her, wiping her tears
While counting the stars shining in Canna's mind
big laughing sound was felt like it could break the window
However, I don't know
what a sigh hidden in time means,
what I am supposed to do with the things disappeared
I ask myself who you are
You have given Canna so much delight and sorrow
but I still don't know who you really are
Furthermore, I also wonder who Canna is, too,
and why she misses you even without knowing who you are

Youn Hea-jeing
Vice-president of Asian Pacific Writers Association. Awarded The 6th Sinmunye Literature Prize. Published poetry book *Ringing a Bell in Longing* and more

칸나는 해법 모색 중

당신의 향기와 느낌이 좋아
당신의 사람이 되었습니다
당신의 눈동자 속에서
미소 짓고 있는 행복한 칸나
당신 또한 활짝 웃고 있어서
칸나는 세상을 다 얻은 것 같았어요
부드러운 손길은 언제나 설레임
함께했던 그 많은 시간들
눈물을 닦아주며 토닥여 주었어요
칸나의 마음밭에 빛나는 별들을 바라보며
웃음소리가 창문을 깨뜨리기도 했지요
그러나 그러나…
시간들 뒤에 숨은 한숨은 무엇인가요
순간 속에 사라진 것들은 어찌하나요
당신은 누구십니까
칸나에게 기쁨과 슬픔을 안겨준
당신은 진정 누구십니까
알 수 없는 당신을 그리워하는
칸나는 또 누구입니까

윤혜정
아태문인협회 부이사
장, 제6회 신문예문학
상 대상 외, 시집 『그리
움이 벨을 울릴 때』 외.

Dokdo Island is Ours

Roaring sounds of dark blue ocean waves
Ah, the sounds of heartbeats of Korea

The island formed with patriotic blood
stands against the country without moral conscience
that tries to pull the waist of the island closer to it

Arteries of white-clad race
pop out with hot blood to protect the island
awakening the patriotic spirits from Mt. Hanla to Mt. Baekdu

Dokdo island is our own, belonging to the territory of Korea
The crashing sounds of the waves against the island
are the sounds of heartbeats of our race,
the breathing sounds of beautiful land of Korea

Lee Kwang-hee
Board member of Korea Sinmunye Literature Association. Awarded Yangchun Writers Association. Literature Prize. Published poetry book *Spring of Goryeosan Mountan* and more

독도는 우리 땅

검푸른 파도 소리
아, 대한민국 심장 소리다

붉은 피로 뭉친 섬
허리 당겨 끌고 가려는
양심 없는 나라도 있다

백의민족 동맥이
뜨거운 피로 섬을 지키려
한라에서 백두까지 깨운다

독도는 대한민국의 땅
섬을 부딪는 울음소리는
우리 민족의 심장 뛰는 소리
삼천리 금수강산 숨소리다

이광희
한국신문예문학회 이사,
양천문인협회문학상 외,
시집 『고려산의 봄』 외.

While Making a Living

While making a living
sometimes we stumble down
where we are supposed not to

Sometimes we talk about love
where we are supposed not to
and shed tears
where we are supposed not to

While making a living
sometimes we have to let go of a lover
to love no more
for the time

After letting go of the things
that are supposed not to be let go of
sometimes we have to live the time
like an animal
being captured in the darkness
while we are making a living

Lee Geun-bae
President of The National Academy of Arts. Poet who won the prizes five times from different annual spring literary contests sponsored by major newspapers in Korea. Awarded Jung Ji-yong Literature Prize and more. Published poetry book, *Songs, Our Songs* and more

살다가 보면

살다가 보면
넘어지지 않을 곳에서
넘어질 때가 있다

사랑을 말하지 않을 곳에서
사랑을 말할 때가 있다
눈물을 보이지 않을 곳에서
눈물을 보일 때가 있다

살다가 보면
사랑하는 사람을
사랑하지 않기 위해서
떠나보낼 때가 있다

떠나보내지 않을 것을
떠나보내고
어둠 속에 갇혀
짐승스런 시간을
살 때가 있다
살다가 보면

이근배
대한민국예술원 원장, 신춘문예 5관왕, 정지용문학상 외, 시집 『노래여 노래여』 외.

A Scenery of the Mountain Village 176

Having lost its mother
a star wandered to find the mother
and took a wrong direction
before it came down onto the earth
and fell asleep
in the well of our house

I made a call
to the home for missing children of the sky
and I was told that the mother was also missing
wandering somewhere to find the lost star

Again taking a look at the star in the well
to see if it is still in sleep
I find the footprints only
looking like shiny water drops
being left in the air
while the star was ascending to the sky

Lee Myung-woo
The first president of The Korean Writers Association, Kyunggi Gwangju Branch. Poet has written 1896 poems with the theme of scenery of mountain village. Published 18 poetry books with the title, *Scenery of Mountain Villages*

산골 풍경 176

엄마 잃은 별 하나가
엄마 엄마 찾다가
가는 길을 잘못 들어
지상으로 내려와
우리 집 우물에서
잠이 들었네

하늘 미아보호소로
전화를 걸었더니
그 엄마도 아기 찾아
헤매인다네

다시 기만
우물을 들여다봤더니
그 사이에 걸어 나와
하늘로 올라간 발자국만
허공에
똑 똑 똑 찍혀있네

이명우
경기도광주문인협회
초대회장, 「산골 풍경」
1,896편 발표, 시집
『산골 풍경』18권

A Love Song of Flowering Dewdrops

In the morning bright and shiny
dewdrops glitter radiantly
between flowers and leaves under the sunlight

Flower buds look soft but bouncy
appearing to have soul for love indwelling in them
Of dewdrops sparkling on the flower petals
appearing sad or delightful
I wonder if they are teardrops hidden behind leaves

A water droplet reminding me of a jade bead
is a mirror of nature projected where we can see
a watercolor painting as if embroidered with the beauty
of nature

On the clean, transparent surface of the dewdrop
seems to be lingering a warm breath
of an oxalis flower making my heart sway

Lee Beom-dong
Member of THe Korean Writers Association. Awarded The 11th Sunmunye Literature Prize.
Published poetry book, *Flowers Covering the Ground Surface*

이슬꽃 연가

해맑은 새 아침
영롱하게 반짝이는 이슬이
꽃과 잎 사이에 햇살처럼 빛난다

탱글탱글 맺힌 꽃망울엔
애잔한 사랑의 영혼이 깃들고
슬픈 듯 기쁜 듯
꽃잎에 맺힌 영롱한 이슬꽃은
파란잎 갈피 속에 감춰진 눈물인가?

옥구슬 같은 물방울은
투영投影한 거울, 그곳엔
자연의 아름다운 수채화가 수놓아 있다

뽀얀 살갗에 남겨진
따뜻한 그 입김, 그것은
내 가슴에 일렁이는 한 송이 사랑초.

이범동
한국문협 회원, 제11회 신문예문학상 수상, 지면꽃시집.

A Train Station Inside Me

Trying not to lose the track
I was anxious, whimpering like a child

The place where you used to be in

In the empty space where you no longer exist
water wells up as in a puddle

Recalling the great time we had together
I find myself getting soaked again in reminiscence

No matter how hard I try to deny the past
the old train station inside me never lets it go

Still staying wet like a foolish lover at the place you left
even after dozens of years have passed

A flower that never withers must be living in the station

Lee Byung-yeon
Member of Korea Women Writers Association. Awarded The 18th Korea Creative Literature Prize. Published poetry book *Hooking a Rock*

내 안의 역驛

사라져가는 꼬리를 놓지 않으려고
나는 어린아이처럼 훌쩍거렸다

당신이 있던 텅 빈 자리

당신이 빠져나간 그 자리에
웅덩이처럼 물이 고이기 시작했다

함께한 결 고운 한때를 떠올리다가
나는 또 젖어 든다

고개를 저을수록 항복할 줄 모르는
내 안의 역

당신이 떠난 역은
수십 년이 지났어도 미련한 애인처럼 젖어 있고

그곳에는 마르지 않는 꽃이 산다

이병연
한국여성문학인회 회원, 제16회 한국창작문학상 대상, 시집 『바위를 낚다』 외.

Snowflakes Blooming like Flowers in Winter

Including the winding pass of Seonjaryeung
the whole mountain is covered with snow

On every twig and branch
snowflakes piled up appear so much attractive

As if competing each other in a contest
boasting their beauty as much as possible

Brightening the world with flower-like snowflakes
making the darkness and despair disappear

Inviting happiness with a chorus of joy
that couldn't be felt happier

Making the world full of delights
with snowflakes blooming like flowers

Lee Bo-young
Professor at Baekseok United Theology Graduate School. Member of The Korean Writers Association. Board member of Quarterly Munye Writers Association.

겨울 눈꽃 피다

선자령 굽이굽이
온 산 눈 덮인

나뭇가지마다
소담하게 핀 꽃이

서로 경쟁하듯 아름답게
꽃단장 뽐내네.

세상을 꽃 피울 때
어둠과 절망도 사라지고

환희의 합창으로
더없는 행복함에

기쁨의 꽃
가득하네.

이보영
백석연합신학신대원 교수, 한국문인협회 회원, 계간문예작가회 이사.

The Forest in May

Following the cries of cuckoos in light green
I have come to the forest to plunge into the ocean in springtime
Only to find that they have already fluttered far away
But still I see the color of mountain getting imbued with green
Where wild roses blooming in white make me long for the first love,
The gentle fragrance of acacia blossoms can be inhaled
Bush warblers sing lightly the songs with a five tone scale
Dandelions reach nirvana with their spores on the heads
Bright yellow celandine flowers are blooming in everywhere.
Today in the sunlight shinning green that comes through the waving branches
I love to lay my heart down in the forest all day long

Lee Bong-woo
Awarded the Prize for Short Poems at Seoul City's Open Contest of Poetry for Screen Door of the Subway. Published poetry book *Drawn to the Look of Eyes*

오월의 숲

봄 바다에 빠지고 싶어 숲으로 갔는데요
뻐꾹새 울음 따라 연두 자락 휘날리며
벌써 저만치 갔습니다.
산빛은 싱그러운 초록으로 물들어가고
하얗게 핀 찔레꽃은 첫사랑 그리움을 불러옵니다.
아카시아 꽃향기는 들숨에 살포시 묻어오고
휘파람새 울음은 오음계로 방울방울 날아갑니다.
까까중 민들레 피안에 들고
노랑꽃 애기똥풀 지천으로 폈습니다.
흔들리는 나뭇잎 사이로 푸른 햇살 반짝이는 오늘
온종일 숲속에 마음을 부려 놓고 싶습니다.

이봉우
서울시 스크린도어 시 공모 당선, 짧은 시 짓기 금상, 시집 『눈빛 끌림으로』

The Drunken Sea

At Seungsanpo Port
Men are more than women
Women are more than men
Similar to the sea
I talk only to myself
The sea talks only to itself
As I drink alcohol
It's the sea that gets drunk
At Seungsanpo Port
The sea gets drunk
More easily all the time

Lee Sang-jin
Born in Seosan, choongnam. Awarded Lee Sang-hwa Literature Prize and more. Published poetry book, *Sunsanpo Port in Longing*

술에 취한 바다

성산포城山浦에서는
남자가 여자보다
여자가 남자보다
바다에 가깝다
나는 내 말만 하고
바다는 제 말만 하며
술은 내가 마시는데
취하긴 바다가 취하고
성산포에서는
바다가 술에
더 약하다

이생진
충남 서산 출생, 이상
화문학상 외, 시집 『그
리운 성산포』 외.

Roses

The sky is burning red
The temperature of my love is hot as such
Longing for you in admiration
my eyes are shining as such
Like molten iron getting heated with the bellow
I am fiery and passionate as such

When you looted my soul
as if occupation forces take the spoils of war
tearing off the red curtains of my heart
exposing the flesh of my body and blinding my eyes
the color of love tempered with purity is as such

Trampling boors in heat rushing closer
my eyes staring at one place only shine as such
The hands being held together there is as such
The light drawn closer to me by your muscle is as such
What I felt kneeling down on my knee towards you is as such

Lee Soon-ock
Vice-president of Modern Literature Trend. Awarded The Prize at Subway Poetry Contest. Published poetry book, *Wolryungga* and more

장미

하늘이 붉게 타오르고 있어
내 사랑의 온도가 저래
당신을 사모하고
흠모하는 내 눈빛이 꼭 저래
순간 달아오른
풀무질 당한 쇳물같이 저래

당신이 점령군으로
내 영혼을 전리품으로 삼았을 때
화들짝 붉은 심장의 휘장이 찢겼지
속살을 보이고 눈이 멀어버린
정금으로 단련된 순정의 색이 바로 저래

달겨드는 잡것들의 발정을 짓뭉개고
오직 한곳을 응시하는 눈빛이 저래
그곳에서 잡은 손길이 저래
당신 힘살로 당겨진 빛이 저래
당신 향해 무릎 굽힌 내 오금이 저래

이순옥
현대문학사조 부회장,
지하철 시 공모전 당
선, 시집 『월영가』 외.

A Streak of Tears

Struggling with the language
mysterious in a poetry book
I tossed and turned in bed for several nights

Awakening in the morning of rainy spring today
poetic dictions came to me one by one
as if breaking the shell and whispering its meaning

Glowing like a morning star
the words broke open the heart
waking me up by shaking my foggy head

Now I take a look at the picture
on the poetry book cover
of the poet whom I didn't know well enough

And finally I see
the poet's language coming alive
all naked in its meanings

Lee Soon-ja
Member of The Korean Writers Association. Awarded many prizes at different writing contests. Published poetry book *Spores Becoming Butterflies*

눈물 한 줄기만

시집 속의
알 수 없는 언어들과
사나흘 밤 뒤척였습니다

오늘 아침 봄비 속삭이는데
껍질 부수고 나온 언어 하나 둘
눈 뜨고 일어섰습니다

샛별 같은 빛을 내며
가슴 틈새 비집기도 하고
멍한 머리 흔들어 깨웠습니다

표지에 실린
알 수 없는 시인의 모습
다시 들여다보았습니다

오늘은
훨훨 벗은 나신裸身
다 보여 주었습니다.

이순자
한국문협 회원, 백일장
다수 당선, 시집『홀씨
되어 나비 되어』

A Proposal of Marriage

Let's just live together for once
You with impaired speech
Me with a hunchback

Let's just live together for once
You having no one to be attached
Me having no one to lay down myself with

Let's just live together for once
You walking with a limp
Me having done time in prison

Let's just live together for once
You suffering leprosy for 10 years
Me suffering leprosy for 5 years

Lee Seung-ha
Made literary debut through *Joong-Ang Daily Newspaper*. Professor at Joong-Ang Univ. Published poetry book, *A Study of Love* and more

구혼

같이 한번 살자꾸나
반벙어리 너랑
곱사등이 나랑

같이 한번 살자꾸나
붙일 데 없는 너랑
얹힌 데 없는 나랑

같이 한번 살자꾸나
다리 저는 너랑
만기 출옥 나랑

같이 한번 살자꾸나
십 년 문둥이 니캉

이승하
1984년 중앙일보 신춘문예 당선, 중앙대학교 교수, 시집 『사랑의 탐구』 외.

Toxic Smog from Factory Chimneys

Toxic smog coming out of factory chimneys
being discharged in combustion incompleted

People are afraid of being exposed
to dioxin existing for decades once it is produced

While people are leaving the factory area
trees fail to grow, losing its color and withering

Growing around the deserted factories
trees still bloom flowers with the cold heart

Environmentally friendly cooperations only
will be surviving even after millennium years

Lee Young-kyoung
Poet, Writer of children's literature. Deputy head of media team at Monthtly Sinmunye. Published poetry book, *Snow Flowers,* and more

굴뚝의 노출

굴뚝에서 뿜어 나오는 검은 독성 연기
불완전한 연소의 노출

수십 년간 존재하는 다이옥신
노출을 자제하길 바라는 사람들

주변의 나무들은 색을 발하고
사람들이 떠나가는 공장

폐허가 된 공장을 덮는 나무들
꽃 피었는데 춥다

환경을 생각하는 기업은 10,000세기 이
후에도
기업가의 자손이 될 수 있다

이영경
시인·아동문학가,
《월간신문예》미디어
차장, 시집 「눈꽃」

Spring Days Are Special

With the hands holding out
inviting happiness

Under the park bench
dandelion flowers blooming with fluffy spores

They can be easily observed anywhere
enough to be called the flowers of spring

Spring days are special with dandelion flowers

Lee Young-mi
Ph. D in education Adjunct professor. Head of Counselling Education Center

봄날은 특별하다

내민 손 가득
행복을 부른다.

공원 벤치 아래
홀씨 활짝 피운 민들레

흔하게 볼 수 있어서
따스한 봄꽃

봄날은 특별하다.

이영미
교육학 박사, 겸임교수,
상담교육센터 센터장.

Azaleas

I wore lipstick in dark red
Don't say I look gaudy but come to see me

My heart feels like it's about to burst
flaring up like a flame inside me

If you don't say anything to me having open mind
you must have a desert in your mind

Try to make a smile
You would feel love pouring out of a spring

Lee Young-ae
Poet, painter. Committee member of traditional literature research of The Korean Writers association. Published poetry book *Breaking the Early Dawn*

영산홍

립스틱 새빨갛게 발랐어요
천박하다 마시고 날 보러 오세요

가슴이 터질 것 같아요
타오르는 이 마음 불꽃입니다

활짝 연 마음에 아무 말 없다면
그대 가슴은 사막입니다

미소라도 지어보세요
그럼 사랑의 샘물이 솟을 겁니다

이영애
시인·화가, 한국문협
전통문학연구위원,
시집 『미명을 깨고』
외.

Folding Clothes

Untangling and straightening washed clothes
twisted and wrinkled to put them in order

Removing the smells of sweat, soil and oil
stained on the clothes that proves a hard time of life
using air refreshener having nice scents
I fold neatly dry and soft clothes in the afternoon
thinking about the day of my family

Cheer up! I talked to myself in my mind
placing the hands one more time
on the clothes my family would wear again later

Lee Ok-jin
Member of the Korean Writers Association. Awarded Achievement Trophy from Kyunggi Writers Association. Published poetry book *The Road*

빨래를 개며

꼬인 곳 바로 놓고
주름진 곳 펴서 차곡히 쌓는다

옷 속에 묻혀 온 고단한 시간의
땀 냄새 흙냄새 기름 냄새
향기 나는 세제로 지우고
보송하게 마른 빨래를 개며
가족의 하루를 가늠해 보는 오후

힘내라
다시 입고 나갈 옷 위에
손길 한 번 더 얹는다

이옥진
한국문인협회 회원,
경기문협 공로상,
시집 『길』

The Ocean

In the chest wide rather than free
feeling contracting muscles
a boat is floating

A wonderful journey
on the waves breathing harshly
for the empty boat floating today
planning to hunt secret treasures

Dreaming to catch the stars
with the fragrance of the empty boat

The ocean in front of me
Thanks to you, Prometheus,
I come to know the stars

Lee En-song
Principle of Songrim middle school. Member of The Korean Writers Association. Awarded Noh Cheon-myeong Literature Prize and more. Published poetry book *City Dweller*.

바다

꿈틀대는 근육
자유보다는 넓은 가슴에
배로 떴다

황홀한 여정
설레는 파도 거친 숨결
오늘만은 빈 배로 떠 그리고
은밀한 보물을 담으리라

빈 배의 공허한 향기로
별을 담으리라

내 앞에 바다
프로메테우스
너로 별을 알게 되었구나

이은송
한국문협 회원, 노천명 문학상 외, 시집 「도시인」 외, 현)송림중학교 교장.

Maidens in Spring

In the spring, dry twigs of willow rejuvenate with flowing sap
The dreams in light green are getting thicker like fog
During the night with the moon shining bright
the moonlight looks intriguing and weird
being shattered on the petals of pear blossoms
when a singing of cuckoo comes faintly
touching the heartstrings of maidens

In spring, maidens suffer heartburn
feeling demurely aroused inside

With the fluttering heart
watching a flower blooming at a distance
listening to the sounds of the wind
passing through the bamboo forest
and to the singing of a nightingale
perching on the branch soaked in water

Strolling around the path secretly placing all their heart
at the branches with cherry blossoms being in full bloom

Lee Eui-young
Board member of Modern Writers Association. Awarded Baekdusan Literature Prize. Published poetry book *The Mind Going for a Path*

봄 처녀

버드나무 마른 가지에 봄물이 돌아
연초록 꿈이 안개처럼 어리는 시절
달 밝은 밤
이화 꽃잎에 부서지는 달빛은
요기롭고
아련히 들리는 두견이 울음소리
심금을 울리면

마음이 달뜬 봄 처녀는
가슴앓이를 시작한다

저만치 핀 한줄기 봄꽃에도
대나무숲을 지나는 바람 소리에도
보슬비 내리는 날
물먹은 가지에서 우는
꾀꼬리 소리에도
가슴 설레이며

흐드러진 벚꽃 가지에
숨은 정 걸어놓고 꽃길을 서성인다

이의영
현대작가회 이사, 백두산문학상 외, 시집 『길 떠나는 마음』 외.

A Song for April

Drinking sorrow in cold dew at dawn
Leaving the countless partings behind
Expecting the first meeting with a hope

Temptation of the breeze tickling the whole body
Irresistible whisperings of the sunlight shining bright
The buds of flowers growing with hopes everyday
Breathing out their liveliness, crouching on the ground

A day in sorrow is felt long, hanging on the branches
Although joy of life is felt to last in such a short time
We are taking steps without being certain of the future

I may have to walk on a journey to places far away
Taking all the wind and the storm or under the starlight
To be something meaningful that wouldn't be forgotten
To be something meaningful that wouldn't be forgotten

Lee In-ae
General Director of Asian Pacific Writers Association. Steering committee member of Insadong Poets Association. Published poetry book *Poems Giving Composure to the Mind*

4월의 노래

서러움 찬이슬에 타서 마신 새벽
헤일수 없는 결별을 뒤로한 채
새로운 포부로 두근대는 첫 만남

언 몸을 간질이는 실바람의 유혹
거부할 수 없는 햇살의 속삭임
웅크린 대지 위에 숨을 토해내듯
나날이 희망으로 부푸는 꽃봉오리

가지마다 널린 슬픔의 날은 길고
생의 희열은 덧없이 짧기만 한데
불확실한 내일을 향해 딛는 발걸음

나 이대로 먼 길을 걸어가야 하리
비바람 별빛에 찰랑이며 찰랑이며
잊히지 않을 의미 있는 무엇이 되리
잊히지 않을 의미 있는 무엇이 되리

이인애
아태문인협회 사무총장, 인사동시인협회 운영이사, 저서 『마음에 평안을 주는 시』 외.

Dandelions

Being trampled in pain
But keeping the wound, though

Sitting right here
After traveling a long distance

Holding the mind puffed up
They speak, opening the mouth
In the shape of a circle

With the head of white spores
On a thin stalk

With painstaking efforts
Making them look as pale as death

With hairs raised up high in breeze
Dandelions bring forth
Fluffy spores looking like a cloud

Lee Je-woo
Board member of JoongAng Univ. Writers Association. Awarded the Prize for the Best 10 Essays in 2023. Published poetry book *Visiting a New Place*

민들레

밟히며 아파하며
그 상처를 지켜내며

생의 먼 거리를
이 강산에 당겨 앉아

사려 쥔
부푼 속내로
동그랗게 말문 연다.

하이얀 씨방머리
한 목청 뽑아놓고

핏기가 가시도록
모지름을 한껏 써서

머리채
틀어올린 채
꽃구름을 피운다.

이제우
중앙대문인회 이사,
2023년 〈좋은수필〉
'베스트에세이 10'
수상, 시집 『초행』

Rain in Spring

At the time for a generation falling into a deep slumber
the whole world gets frozen in solemn silence;
when the period of mourning for forty nine days ends
white mourning clothes are gathered and put into fire
A life being vaporized into the sky leaving ashes only
would be turned into water again in the air
and come down to the ground soaking new lives
Taking nutritious elements inherited from earlier generation
new sprouts grow on the slash-and-burn field
to bring forth the buds of flowers on the branches
Perishing lives don't just end up dead in vain
They become manure for next generations
embracing new life forms with their sacrifice
That's a life circle in which I would be born again
being soaked in the amniotic fluid of the womb

Lee Ju-sig
Made literary debut through Munyesajo in 2013. Member of Asian Pacific Writers Association. Published poetry book *Waves of the Moonlight*

봄비

한 세대가 잠드는 시간
엄숙한 침묵에 온 세상이 동결되어
사십구일 간의 의식을 끝내고
소복을 주섬주섬 거두어 불태운다
한 세대의 재를 남기고 하늘로 간 수증기는
교합으로 양수가 되어 내려와
새로운 생명을 촉촉이 적신다
전 세대의 자양분을 먹고
화전에 움트는 씨앗
가지로 솟구치는 꽃망울
소멸은 죽음이 아니다
거름이 되는 것이다
새로운 생명을 감싸는 깃이다
모태의 양수에 흠뻑 젖어
나는 새로 태어난다

이주식
2013년 문예사조 등단, 아태문협 회원, 시집 『달빛 물결』

Farming

To my surprise, some sweet potatoes have grown well
To my disappointment, some sweet potatoes have grown poorly

I feel sorry for both of them
for I haven't paid equal attentions to them somehow

Regretting that I should have raised them
to fit in their need
not to fit in my greed

Harvesting sweet potatoes
I couldn't help thinking about my children

Lee Joon-hee
Board member of Korea Modern Poets Association. CEO of Handysoft Inc. Published poetry book *Parting with Dewdrops*

농사

어떤 건 웃기게 실하고
어떤 건 슬프게 비실해

마음을 못 써 미안하고
마음을 더 써 미안하다

적당한 네 몸집 맞춰
적당한 내 욕심으로
키웠더라면

고구마를 캐면서
자꾸 아이 생각이 난다

이준희
한국현대시인협회 이사, 주)핸디소프트 대표이사, 시집 『이슬로 이별을 한다』 외.

On a Day like This

After having melt the frozen heart
with flowers fully bloomed
now being a wing of the spring breeze
a plum blossom lightly flies in the sky
becoming the wind of the day

Putting her life in a roll with ingredients in a laver
'I can't live with money in my pocket' she always said,
keeping her pocket empty to donate money to charity;
now having made the branches of a tree bloom with blossoms
*Mrs. Choon-ja falls like a flower petal

On a day like this, I like to take a long breath
having a cup of coffee idly
putting bright sunlight in it and stirring it slowly

*Mrs. Choon-ja is an old lady known for the donation of money she made selling a fast food called Kimbap during her entire life

---

Lee Chang-sik
Former elementary school principal. Awarded the 9th Heidegger Literature Prize. Published poetry book, *Clues of Thoughts*

이런 날도 있다

언 가슴 녹이고
꽃타령 드높더니
한 점 봄바람의 날개 되어
하늘하늘 하늘을 난다
매화가 바람 되는 날

삶을 김밥으로 말아
'돈을 두고는 못 살겠더라'
빈 주머니를 기부로 채운 일상
손발의 가지에 붉은 꽃 피우고서
춘자* 씨가 꽃잎으로 지는 날

은빛 햇살
커피잔에 저어
쉬엄쉬엄 심호흡 하고픈 날

이창식
전 초등학교교장, 하이
데거문학상, 시집 『생
각꼬투리』

*열 살부터 아흔다섯까지 평생 김밥 말아 기부한
박춘자 할머니 이야기

A Nest for Birds

I made a nest for birds
on a persimmon tree at the back yard

A pair of bushtits
flew in the nest to live there

They wake me up every morning
with friendly songs they sing for me

As if paying the rent instead
for living there
for free

Lee Cheol-woo
Member of Tthe Korean Writers Association. Awarded Marine Literature Prize and more.
Published the collection of sijo *Wondangi Hill* and more

새집

뒤뜰 감나무에
새집 하나 만들었다

곤줄박이 한 쌍이
들어와 살았다

정겨운 노래로
아침마다 나를 깨운다

집세가
없어서인지
노래로 대신한다

이철우
한국문인협회 회원, 소년해양문학상 외, 시조집 『원댕이고개』 외.

A Path by the River

On a path by the river
cosmos flowers were swaying in the breeze
just making smiles in silence
showing the petals getting blushed in shyness

In the shadow of you
who have left me
I walk in the dusk, trying to read
the meaning of the time we had been together

Whisperings once gone
are coming back in echo
to the empty places
where you still remain but only in my memory

Lee Han-jae
Member of The Korean Writers association. Awarded Prize at National-wide Creative Poetry Contest. Published poetry book *Stepping Stones* and more

강변 오솔길

코스모스 하늘거리던
강변 오솔길
너는 말없이 웃기만 했었지
수줍음으로 발그레 물들었던
그날의 꽃잎들

이제는 떠나버린
너의 그림자 속에서
일몰을 밟으며
그날을 읽는다

멀어져간 속삭임은
메아리로 돌아오고
텅 빈 자리에
너는 또 한없이 가득하고

이한재
한국문인협회 회원,
전국창작시 공모 수상,
시집 『징검다리』 외.

Asking Pardon

It's all my fault
His voice sounded deep and hoarse
like those of stream water stopped to flow
Sorry. Forgive me
Watching his blank stares
filling the air
I wanted to sit down right there
feeling like I would rather disappear
I should have asked pardon first
for everybody knew he didn't do anything wrong
While asking pardon for me on my behalf
he gets on his head the sunset falling like a choir in tears
Although I learned there is proper time for everything
I realize I have already lost the time

Lee Hyang-ah
Made literary debut through *Hyundaimoonhak*. Adviser of International PEN, Korea Center.
Published poetry book, *A Pilgim's Letter*

사죄 謝罪

모두 내 잘못이야
그의 목소리가 잠겨 있었다
흐르다 멈춘 개울물같이
미안해, 용서해 줘
아무것도 겨냥하지 않은 그의 눈길이
대기 속에 가득 차오르는 동안
나는 차라리 그 자리에 주저앉아
없어지고 싶었다
내가 먼저 사죄할 걸
그가 잘못하지 않았음은 세상이 다 알 것이다
나를 대신 빌고 있는 그의 머리 위에
합창처럼 쏟아지는 저녁노을 목울음
모든 것은 때가 있음을 배웠는데도
나는 이미 시간을 놓쳤다

이향아
《현대문학》등단, 국제 PEN 한국본부 고문, 시집 『순례자의 편지』 등 25권.

My Mother Filling Up My Mind

I walk in April

On a day my mother got sick
taking a stroll along the path across a field
I picked the shoots of mugwort emerging in clusters
to make a soybean paste soup with mugwort in it;
having the soup with cooked rice
my mother said in a low voice, 'this tastes good'

Now with my mother no longer with us
mugworts only grow fast and wild
taking all over the green fields

No longer I pick the shoots of mugwort to deliver
the scent of spring gathered from the wild

Lee Hyun-kyung
Member of Korea Sinmunye Literature Association. Awarded The 20th Tammi Literature Prize and more. Published poetry book *A Mediation Bloomed in Clarity*

어머니가 차오른다

사월을 걷습니다

어머니 몸져누우신 날
답답한 마음에 들길을 걷다가
무더기로 파릇하게 올라온 쑥을 뜯어서
된장을 풀어 쑥국을 끓였습니다
국에 밥을 돌돌 말아 드시며
낮은 소리로 '맛나다' 하십니다

그날 이후, 어머니는 보이질 않고
초록 들판에 거침없이
쑥쑥 자라난 쑥이 지천입니다

봄의 서식지에서 채집한 쑥의 향기
이젠 건넬 수가 없습니다

이현경
한국신문예문학회 회원
제20회 탐미문학상 외,
시집 『맑게 피어난 사색』

Daffodils

Missing you
I planted a few daffodils
beside a stone wall

Surviving cold winter
being deeply rooted in the frozen ground
the daffodils bear bulbous flowers
every year without fail

Like your constant love
and your fragrance as well

Lost in the fragrance
I have nothing
but love for you

Lee Hye-sook
Professor at Jeju Medical School. Awarded the 12th Esprit Literature Prize. Published poetry book *The Name, Moher* and more

수선화

그대 보고 싶어
돌담 옆에
수선화 몇 포기 심었다

찬 겨울 언 땅에
알뿌리 깊이 박고
해마다 어김없이
꽃피운다

변치 않는 그대 사랑처럼
변치 않는 그대 향기처럼

그 향기에 취한 나
어찌 그대를
사랑하지 않으리.

이혜숙
제주대학교 의과대학 교수, 제12회 에스프리 문학상, 시집 『그 이름, 어머니』 외.

If Love Gets Thicker

If love gets thicker
Can it bear fruits?

The more I miss in my heart
The louder I hear me cry like an owl all night long

The figure that comes to my mind
Turns around to rush
into my heart for an embrace

Whereabouts I wonder our love is building a house

Yi Ho-yeon
Poet. Ph.D. in literature. Vice-president of Korea Civil Servants Literature Association. Published poetry book *Dialogues in Coral Color*

사랑이 짙어지면

사랑이 짙어지면
열매로 맺히던가

그릴수록 짙어가는 이 그리움은
한밤 내내 부엉이 소리로 울고

떠오르는 모습은
빙그르르 내어달아
내 가슴에 안기는데

우리 사랑 어디쯤 고운 집을 지을까

이호연
시인·문학박사, 한국공무원문협 부회장, 공무원문학상, 시집 『산호빛 대화』 외.

A Storage of Sorrow

The cracking sounds of gun fire are coming through white smog

Dogs are barking outside with bloody eyes

Armored vehicles push away the evening in despair

Flesh and blood resisting in the blankets

Silent flowers kept in dozens of layers of time

A piece of human flesh buried in the ground

Wriggling itself with the head towards tomorrow

Who dares say there is no spring in Ukraine?

Lee Hyo
 Member of Thte Korean Writers Association at Nohwon Branch Awarded The 5th Asian Pacific Writers Association Literature Prize. Published poetry book, *A Breath of Yours*

슬픔의 창고

총탄 소리가 하얗게 내린다

밖에는 개 짖는 소리가 붉다

장갑차는 저녁을 밀고 절망을 연다

저항하는 담요 안의 속살들

수십 겹의 시간 속에서 침묵하는 꽃

떨어진 살점 하나, 땅속에 묻혀

꿈틀거리며 머리로 내일을 든다

누가, 우크라이나의 봄은 없다 말하는가

이 효
한국문인협회 노원지부 회원, 제5회 아태문학상 수상, 시집 『당신의 숨 한 번』

A Journey of Life

Coming out
of pitchy darkness

Passing a labyrinth of time
mysterious for a birth

Going through delight and sorrow,
despair and joy, desire and conflicts

Sailing in predicament with no turning back
towards the maze-like places unknown to us

Even in oblivious time
still longing for the beautiful memories of the past

Facing the stormy apocalypse
we find a spiritual rest in trusting God

Lee, Hee-bok
Poet, essayist. Board member of International PEN, Korea Center. Awarded Korea Christian Poetry Prize. Published poetry book *Longing & Love* and more

삶의 여정

흑암에서
한 줄기 빛으로

탄생의 신비로운
시간의 미로를 지나

기쁨과 슬픔, 절망과 환희
욕망과 갈등의 세월을 헤치고

이희복
시인·수필가, 국제PEN
한국본부 이사,
한국기독시문학 작품상,
시집 『그리움과 사랑』
외.

미지의 운명으로 향하는
회항할 수 없는 고난의 항해

망각의 세월에도 아름다웠던
추억들을 그리움으로 사위며

종말의 폭풍이 몰아쳐도
믿음으로 안식을 얻는다

Me, Being Pacified

Feeling loneliness, I go to a forest
Talking to the trees
I become the forest

Feeling sad, I go to the sea
Listening to the roaring sounds of waves
I become the waves

Feeling longing inside me, I go to a river
Listening to the whisperings of the river water
I flow in the water following the river

Feeling like to cry, I write poems with the flowers of tears
Crying out loud with the poems for a while
I become a poem, and the poem becomes me

Feeling like to see someone, I climb a mountain
What I find at the top of the mountain is a rock
Having arrived there earlier, waiting for me

Lim Bo-Seon
Made literary debut through *Monthly Literature* in 1991. Awarded Tthe 29th Overseas Korean Literature Prize and more. Published poetry book *Temperature of My Love is 350℃ and more*

나, 어르기

외로울 땐 숲으로 간다
나무들과 얘기하다 보면
나도 숲이 된다

슬플 땐 바다로 간다
파도의 함성을 듣다 보면
나도 파도가 된다

그리울 땐 강으로 간다
강물의 속삭임 듣다 보면
나도 강 따라 흐른다

울고 싶을 땐 눈물꽃으로 시를 쓴다
한참을 시속에서 울다 보면
난 시가 되고 시는 내가 된다

보고 싶을 땐 산을 오른다
올라가 보니 나보다 먼저 온
바위가 기다리고 있었다

임보선
1991년 《월간문학》 등단, 제29회 동포문학상 외, 시집 『내 사랑은 350℃』 외.

Rain and Coffee

Watching the rain
falling in drops and splattering

I become calm for no reason
wondering if there is someone
who can listen to a small story of mine

The rain
flows in longing
hiding into the darkness

Beyond the misty window
at the same place
that always used to be taken
no one sits there any more

If only there is a cup of coffee
smelling so good with the rich fragrance
I wouldn't mind the rain
pouring down through the night

Im So-ri
poet, pianist, art planner, ocarina player. Steering committee member of Asian Pacific Writers Association.

비와 커피

후두둑
흩어지는 빗살을 보면

까닭없이 차분한 마음
나의 작은 이야기
들어줄 이 누구 없나요

흐르는 비
그리움 되어
어둠 속으로 숨어 버리고

김 서린 투명 유리 넘어
늘 있던
그 자리에 있어 줄 이
지금 아니 없어도

그윽한 커피향이
함께 머물러 준다면
밤새도록 내리는 비라도
나는 싫지 않을 테요

임소리
시인·피아니스트, 예술
기획가, 오카리나연주
자, 아태문인협회 운영
위원.

Taegeukgi of Independence

The shout of hurrays all over the beautiful land of Korea
Crying out of overwhelming emotion of joy with tears
Mountains. streams, plants, and trees, everything in delight
Even taegeukgi, the Korean flag flattering in great joy

Not only do we remember but also the whole world knows
Korea following the reason, fighting for freedom and justice
Living in freedom, pursuing the world peace in harmony
Now the world sopports us doing our best to keep humanity

Arirang, the traditional song we have been singing together,
People around the world know the song and are big fans of K-POP
Representing freedom and peace, Korean Wave is getting popular
Giving people all over the world laughs and clappings of happiness

Yim Choong-bin
Poet, essayist. Advisor of The Korean Writers Association at Ansung branch. Published poetry book *Tasting Like Soy Bean Paste*

광복의 태극기

금수강산 진동하던 만세 함성
감격에 겨워 흘리던 눈물
산천초목도 함께 기뻐하며
힘차게 펄럭이는 태극기까지

우리는 기억한다 세계가 안다
순리를 지킨 자유 정의의 KOREA
평화, 자유와 더불어 잘 산다
지금 세계가 우릴 응원한다

우리가 합창하던 아리랑을
이제 세계가 K-POP으로 열광한다
자유와 평화, 웃음과 박수 속에
한류가 지구촌 곳곳을 누빈다

임충빈
시인·수필가, 한국문협
안성지부 고문, 시집
『장 맛처럼』 외.

A Dream in Spring

During the winter tightly closed
through a pinhole
a sprout sees a tiny little space

The freezing cold winter disappears
without leaving any trace
if a little new bud begins to grow

Going into the space left open for more
the bud dreams to achieve
as much as it wants

The dream in spring becomes a tree
inviting birds to fly down
hoping to make people smile in happiness

Lim Ha-cho
President of Seoul Poets Association. Awarded The Poem of the Year Prize from Monthly Poetry. Published poetry book *Riding a Seesaw*

봄꿈

촘촘하게 꽉 찬 겨울
바늘구멍 사이로
새싹이 본 공간

하늘 무너져 내릴 추위도
여린 새싹 한 잎 솟으면
흔적 없이 사라진다

어떤 꿈을 꾸어도 좋은
욕심껏 안아도
더 많이 남은 공간

봄꿈은 나무가 되고
새가 오고
사람들이 웃는 꿈을 꾼다

임하초
서울시협 시인문학회 회장, 월간 '시' 올해의 시인상 본상, 시집 『나는 시소를 타고 있다』 외.

The First Name
− A nickname for the baby bump in Korean Wave

Blessing, Love, Little Man, Soldier, etc
Babies are given nicknames even before they are born
The first names of the babies while they are in fetus

The babies with the heartbeats in the womb
Being considered to be human beings with humanity
From the traditional perspective of the Korean
Since they become one year old at the moment of the birth

Blessing a new life with the nickname for the baby bump
With love and joy for the baby of the parents
Wishing the baby to grow well and strong with the nickname

All the mothers and fathers in the world choose
The first names of their babies with the best wishes,
The nicknames for the baby bump

Jang jin-ju
Professor at the dept. of open major, Yuhan Univ. Awarded the 23rd Munyesajo Prize. Published many books with co-authors.

첫 이름
― 태명 한류를 꿈꾸다

축복이, 사랑이, 쑥쑥이, 튼튼이, 장군이…
세상에 나기 전부터 이름을 선물 받았나니
태에 있을 때 지어주신 아기의 첫 이름

잉태하면서부터 심장박동은 쉬지 않고
뛰노라
이미 인격적 존재요, 생명이라
세상에 "응애"하고 나면서부터 한 살이 되는
한국의 전통 나이

온 마음 다해 생명을 축복하는 이름,
사랑으로 열매 맺은 기쁨의 이름,
쑥쑥 크고 튼튼하게만 자라 달라는 기원,

온 세상 엄마, 아빠의 소망을 오롯이 담아
부르는
그 이름
태명

장진주
유한대학교 자유전공학과 교수, 제23회 문예사조문학상, 공저 다수.

Mt. Baekdu

Ah, here is the northern end of the land with the sun rising
where mysterious aura of the universe seems to be pervading,
Mt. Baekdu has been observing our history for 10 thousand years
with sixteen peaks surrounding the crater lake on top of it

The mountain was a lifeline of human civilization
The origin of ancient culture full of vitality
Where Hwanwoong, the son God, coming down from the sky
To the place of the sacred tree, set up a new city with his followers

Dangun, the son of Hwanwoong then built at Asadal
The nation of splendid morning with humanitarian ideology
In order to benefit people living well in the world
Making everything in nature, even the East Sea, dance in joy

Lighting up the torch in the harmony of Heaven-Earth-Human
Cultivating human civilization with the help of the sky and the earth
Echoing across the five oceans and the six continents
We will accept different people and their cultures with the open mind

---

Jang Hae-ik
Poet, essayist. Honorary president of Korea Sinmunye Literature Association. Awarded Korean-China Culture and Arts Prize and more. Published books including *A Life Worthy of a 100 Won Coin* and more

백두산

아! 여기 해 돋는 땅 끄트머리
하늘과 맞닿은 우주의 신비 서린 곳
일만 년 역사의 흐름을 지켜본
열여섯 봉우리 천지를 품고 있구나

인류문화의 젖 줄기
새 생명이 넘치는 한 밝달 문화의 발상지
하느님 아들 환웅이 하늘 열어
강림한 신단수 신시에 배달민족 모으시고

환웅의 아들 단군이 아사달에
빛나는 아침의 나라 세워
홍익인간 이화세계의 뜻을 펴니
산천초목 환호하고 동해물도 춤추었어라

천지인의 조화 속에 횃불 밝혀
하늘과 땅 인류문명 계발하여
오대양 육대주 웅비의 메아리로
드넓은 가슴 열어 인류 포용하리라.

장해익
시인·수필가, 한국신문
예문학회 명예회장, 한
중문화예술 대상 외,
저서『백원짜리 인생』
외.

Food

Food manifests the history of our life
Under what circumstances, with whom
and when you have a meal
or what you feel while having a meal
what food you have, all these define who you are
Likewise, all these define who I am

Family members eat the rice steamed in the same cooker
along with affection for the family contained in the meal
In the meal for family breakfast prepared
with the whole heart for the health of the family
ingredients like love and care are also put together
Food the family eats is not only for survival but for love of life

To a friend we haven't met for quite a while
making a cordial conversation even for the sake of convenience
I like to hear someone say "Let's go out to eat sometime"
Even if we eat bread and drink coffee or even if it's just a saying,
I like to hear someone say "Let's go out to eat sometime"

Jeon Min
Board member of International PEN, Korea Center. Awarded Korea Modern Poets Prize.
Published poetry book *A Landscape Painting in Motion*

밥

삶은 밥의 역사다
어떤 상황에서 어떤 밥을
누구와 언제 함께 먹었는지
어떤 마음과 기분으로 먹었는지
네 밥의 역사는 네 삶의 역사이고
내 밥의 역사는 내 삶의 역사다

식구는 한솥밥을 먹는다
한솥에 소복하게 쌓인 정
가족을 위해 정성 들여 지은
따뜻한 아침밥 한 그릇 속에
사랑의 온기가 솔솔 배어있는
밥은 삶의 생존이자 사랑이다

오랜만에 만난 지인에게
정감 어린 대화의 인사치레로
정해진 날짜는 비록 없더라도
언제 우리 만나 밥 한번 먹자
비록 빵이나 커피를 먹더라도
빈말이라 할지라도 밥 한번 먹자

전 민
국제펜한국본부 이사,
한국현대시인상 외,
시집 『움직이는 풍경화』 외.

Bibimbob, Traditional Korean Meal

During the period of impoverishment of late spring in the 1940s
having a short life expectance in average and not enough food
we used to greet people in the morning
"Have you slept well?" or "Have you eaten the breakfast?" These
questions were the casual greetings to the elderly
and the same questions were made to the children, too.

After boiling barleys in a large cauldron to make Bibimbob we put
the cooked barleys into the woven reed basket to cool off
and took out a scoop of them to eat at mealtimes

With Bibimbob made by mixing the boiled barleys, red pepper paste
along with boiled radish green, seasoned wild vegetables
eating green chilli peppers dipped in red pepper paste
we could fill the empty stomachs, and it tasted so good

We got food supplies improved in the 2000s
The meal we used to eat earlier became diversified in kinds
and known as Bibimbob, the best food to the people around the world

---

Jun Yeoung-mo
Member of The Korean Writers Association. Awarded The 9th Modern Poetry Prize. Published poetry book *Memory of Time*

비빔밥

940년대 보릿고개 시절
평균수명이 짧고 먹거리가 부족했을 때
아침 인사로 안녕히 주무셨습니까?
진지(식사) 드셨습니까? 하는 인사가 최고
였고 아이들에겐 밥 먹었느냐고 묻는 것이
인사였지

보리쌀을 한 솥 삶아 통풍이 잘 되는
광주리에 담아 설강에 얹어 두고
끼니때마다 조금씩 덜어 밥을 지었지

꽁보리밥에 고추장 넣고 쓱쓱 비벼
시래기나 산나물 무침 매콤한 풋고추에
된장 꾹 찍어 배고픔을 달래 주었던
최고의 비빔밥이었는데

이천 년대 한층 업그레이드 되어
콩나물비빔밥, 산채비빔밥 등 전국의 비빔
밥이 세계인이 선호하는 최고의 기호
음식이 되었지

전영모
한국문인협회 회원, 현대시 제9회 작품상 외, 시집 『시간의 기억』 외.

A Flower of Love

At the time you are in deep sleep
how pathetic I am being awake like this
If staying up all night, thinking about you only,
I wonder if it would make our love grow
If I drop some teardrops into the joy I feel
I wonder if it would make our love grow
big enough to bear flowers
You, chaste flower,
bloom gorgeously
in the dream of someone sleeping
bloom in pure white form
in my heart trying to sleep in vain

Jun Jong-moon
Former president of Korea Christian Writers Association. Awarded Beautiful Literature Prize.
Published poetry book *The Self-portrait in the Day Being Pale* and more

사랑의 꽃

당신이 곤하게 잠들어 있을 이 시간에
무슨 청승으로 나는 깨어 있는가
이렇게 당신만을 생각하며 밤을 새우면
우리의 사랑은 자라는 걸까
떠오르는 기쁨에
눈물방울도 조금 떨어트리면
사랑은 곱게 자라 꽃을 피울까
소박한 꽃이여
이 밤에 곤하게 잠든 이의 꿈에
화사하게 피어나거라
순백하게 피어나거라
잠들지 못한 내 가슴에도

전종문
한국크리스천문학가협
회 회장 역임, 아름다운
문학상 외, 시집 『창백
한 날의 자화상』 외.

The Wind Blowing at the Crater Lake

The crater lake in jade green
at the highest peak of Mt. Baekdu

The cold wind blows very hard
with the soul of our nation
making the roaring sounds so majestic

The wind having spiraled up
to the top of the sacred mountain
disappears with no traces
into the shade of the blue clouds
leaving mysterious sounds only

And nobody has yet seen
the wind
blowing to nowhere

Jeon ji-myeong
Ph. D. in politics. Adjunct professor at Donggook Univ. Advisory committee member of The Korean Writers Association. Awarded Korea Literary Critics Association Prize.

천지天池의 바람

높고도 높은
저 비췻빛 하늘 못池이여

민족의 혼魂 실은
저 칼바람이 희살칠 때는
눈부신 소리 장엄하도다

성산聖山에 치솟는
저 바람은
신비로운 소리만 남기고
푸른 빛 구름 그늘 속으로
사라진다

누구도
아직 그 바람을
본 적이 없다.

전지명
동국대학교 정치학박사
겸임교수. 한국문학비
평가협회 작가상, 한국
문협 자문위원.

Seeing through a Dewdrop as a Magnifying Glass

I see through a dewdrop as a magnifying glass
the green forest waving in the mountain at a distance
where a poor poet lives
like mountain birds
cleaning their beaks at tree branches
singing songs for the morning

In the pupils of the poet's eyes as clean as the sky
I see the heaven he would fly up to with the fluttering wings

Jung Soon-young
President of Dongmyung Univ. Vice-president of International PEN, Korea Center. Awarded SEjong Culture &Arts Prize. Published poetry book *Are Poems Flowers?*

이슬방울 돋보기로 들여다보니

창틀에 맺힌 이슬방울 돋보기로
진초록 물결치는 건넛산 숲을 들여다보니
산새처럼
둥지 앞 나뭇가지에 부리를 닦고
아침을 노래하는
가난한 시인의 모습이 보이네.

하늘처럼 해맑은 시인의 눈동자 속에
날개 푸득거려 훨훨 날아갈 천국이 보이네.

정순영
동명대학교 총장, 국제
pen한국본부 부이사
장, 세종문화예술대상,
시집 『시는 꽃인가』
외.

A Broken Clock

Tossing and turning at night
She has lived, walking a single path, though

Letting us know proper time
Pointing what's necessary or not
Teaching the wisdom to live a life

Stroking the heads of twelve sisters
Singing lullabies
To put us in sleep

Getting old and weak
But still going on and off
Until she eventually have to stop and lie down

Cheong Young-lye
Member of The Korean Writers Association. Awarded Imaginary Inquiry Writer Prize and more.
Published poetry book *A Salt Flower*

고장 난 시계

밤잠 설치며
외길만 걸으셨다

때를 알려주고
긴말 짧은 말 짚어가며
세상 살아가는 이치도 가르쳤다

열두 자매 머리 쓰다듬고
자장가로
재워 주던 손길

기력 쇠해
가다 서다 가다 시다
끝내는 누우셨다.

정영례
한국문협 회원, 상상탐
구작가상 외, 시집 『소
금꽃』 외.

Everyone Becomes a Poet in Autumn

Everyone becomes a poet in Autumn
writing a poem of gratitude, watching the sky without a dark cloud
writing a poem watching the yellow fields waving in the winds,
watching tinged leaves burning in red and a leaf floating on the stream crystal clear in a valley, thinking about the close of a life

Everyone becomes a poet in Autumn
writing a poem smelling the breath of a mountain welcoming the cool breeze that pushes the hot wind away, seeing the lonely moon
looking down with the pale face of gardenia flowers in the night sky,
writing a poem with the desire to go beyond the horizon with the fluttering heart felt in longing and reminiscence

Everyone becomes a poet in Autumn
Everyone becomes a poet in Autumn

Jeong Yeong-sook
Poet, essayist, writer of children's literature. Awarded Golyeo Literature Prize. Published 12 books and more

가을은 누구나 시인입니다

가을은 시인입니다
먹구름 없는 파-란 하늘만 바라봐도
감사의 시를 씁니다
갈바람에 물결치는 노란 들판을 바라봐도
감사의 시를 씁니다
빨갛게 불타는 단풍과 유리같이
맑은 계곡에 떠내려가는 낙엽 한 잎을
바라보면 인생의 마지막을 생각게 하여서
감사의 시를 씁니다

정영숙
수필가·아동문학가·시인, 고려문학 대상, 저서 12권 외.

가을은 시인입니다
더위 바람 쫓아버리고 산들바람 환영하는
산의 입김만 맡아도 시를 씁니다
밤하늘에 치자꽃 같은 하얀 얼굴로 내려다
보는 무언의 고독한 달을 봐도 시를 씁니다
지평선 넘어 수평선 넘어 어딘가 가고 싶은
 낭만에 시를 씁니다
그리움과 추억이 한 편의 드라마로 가슴을
설레게 해서 시를 씁니다

가을은 누구나 시인입니다
가을은 누구나 시인입니다.

CORONA 19, I Ask for Your Return to Where You Came from

I wonder if CORONA 19 is the death angel sent by Lord
It was so resentful during the pandemic period and I blamed it
for the suffering of neighbors and the loss of my friends

After the pandemic period, awaking from the nightmares
now we have realized that wealth and fame we have been pursuing
with self-interest and greed are all futile delusions

When the Arctic's sea ice melted
wild forests in Australia burned in flames
dead fish were found en masse in the streams
we didn't take them as a warming against our greed

After experiencing how terrible consequence CORONA 19 brought us
we had to think about ourselves being a part of the natural world
about how greedy we have been while ignoring the natural order
and finally have realized we all live in the community of fate

Oh, we have learned the most valuable lesson from you, CORONA 19
Please, return to where you came from as soon as possible

Jung Yong-kyu
Member of The Korean Writers Association & Korea Modern Poets Association. Awarded The 13th Sam Literature Special Work Prize. Published poetry book *A Traveler in Autumn*

코로나19, 조기 귀환을 빌다

코로나19, 그대는 하느님의 사자使者인가
이웃들이 병상에 들고 친구가 하늘나라로 사라
질 때 너무나 두렵고 참으로 원망스러웠다네

시간이 흐르고 악몽에서 점차 깨어나면서
자리自利 탐욕 쫓아 그토록 추구하던 부·귀·영·화
부질없는 허상들이었음을 이제야 알게 된다네

북극에 빙하가 사라지고
호주 원시림이 화염에 휩싸이며
하천엔 물고기들 떼죽음 당하는 경고에도
지구인들 오만방자 반성할 줄 몰랐었지

생명체들은 자연이 삶의 터전인 것을
그대가 연출하는 생생한 현장을 목격하고
순리를 멀리한 채 역리를 탐했는지 돌아보면서
우리 모두 공동운명체인 것을 깨닫게 되는구나

오~호! 그대여, 이제 지구인들 깨달은 바 크니 더
이상 지체하지 마시고 휑하니 귀환하소서.

정용규
한국문협·현대시협 회원, 제13회샘문학상 특별작품상, 시집 『가을 나그네』

My Wife Became a Bird

Holding my hands tightly
you said you were going to be a bird
flying around the world to the end

I pour a cup of rice wine

Birds of unknown names are crying in the forest
You are crying out loud calling for me
but I can neither figure out which sound is yours
nor understand what you are saying

I am just all alone
standing in front of your grave

Jung Jung-nam
Member of Korea Modern Poets Association. Awarded The 13th Sinmunye Literature Prize.
Published poetry book *A Rainbow on a Rear Mirror*

새가 된 아내

당신은 내 손을 꼬옥 쥐고서
죽어서는 새가 될 거라고
이 세상 끝까지 날아다닐 거라고

막걸리 한잔을 부어 놓습니다.

숲속에서는 이름 모를 새들이 울어 댑니다.
당신은 내가 온 줄 알고 날 부르지만
나는 어느 새가 당신인지 알 수가 없습니다.
당신의 이야기도 알아들을 수가 없습니다.

나는 그냥 당신 무덤 앞에
혼자입니다.

정정남
현대시인협회 회원, 제 13회 신문예문학상, 시집 『백미러 속의 무지개』

Hangeul, Launched into the sky

The only alphabet that king created
In harmony with ten vowels and fourteen consonants
With all his loving heart for the people
As new yet easy alphabets it's wiggling

Seeking for the roots of culture from
'Yin-Yang & Five Elements of the Universe'
Mothered on Heaven-Earth-Human,
the Korean alphabet is given birth
By folding the wings of philosophy, Hangeul that comes to life

At the typing speed, At the UNESCO's Memory of the World Resister
As joining the best of rows at the World Alphabet Olympics
The most scientific alphabet open the future
All roads lead to Hangeul

With inheriting the lofty vision of Sejong the Great
As trying the wings of Hangeul that the future generations will keep
Hangeul, launched into the sky, it soars toward the world

Jeong Hae-ran
Member of International PEN, Korea Center
Awarded 'Hwang Jin-Yi Literature Prize' and more
Published poetry book 「A Wind that opens up time」and more

한글, 쏘아 올리다

왕이 만든 유일한 문자
홀소리 10자, 닿소리 14자의 만남
백성 사랑하는 마음 오롯이 담아
쉬우면서도 새로운 글자로 꿈틀거린다

문화의 뿌리는 '음양오행'에서 찾고
하늘, 땅, 사람을 모태로 글자 풀어내
철학의 날개 접고 태어난 한글

자판 입력 속도도, 유네스코에도
문자 올림픽에서도 금빛 꼭대기
가장 과학적인 글자가 여는 미래
모든 길은 한글로 통한다

세종대왕 높은 뜻 이어받아
후손들이 지킬 한글의 날개 펼쳐
세계를 향해 쏘아 올리다

정해란
국제 PEN 한국본부 회원, 제22회 '황진이 문학상' 최우수상 외. 저서 제3시집 『시간을 여는 바람』 외.

Pain

I hear
a sweet whispering
"Love your neighbor like yourself"

You came to me
to live with me
for you liked me

I want to send you away
but still I hear you whisper
"I like to live with you"

You keep telling me
you like me enough to live with me
Well, then, let's live together

Until you decide to leave me alone

Cho Kyu-soo
Poet, essayist. Secretary general of Korea Modern Poets Association. Awarded Peasant's Literature Prize. Published poetry book, *Stars Have Soared*

통증 痛症

나에게 들려오는 달콤한
속삭임
"네 이웃을 내 몸과 같이 사랑하라"

내가 좋아
나와 함께 살고 싶어
나를 찾아온 그놈

멀리 보내고 싶지만
지금도 들려오는
"너와 함께 살고 싶어"

그래 너도 내가 좋아
나에게 왔으니
함께 살아보자

네가 나를 멀리할 때까지

조규수
시인·수필가, 한국현대
시인협회 사무총장, 농
민문학상, 시집『별이
솟았다』 외.

Coming out as a Flower

The sounds of his breathing are like an outcry
just coming out of a long tunnel
With the scale starting from the lowest C
overcoming ten octaves, his breathing sounds
like resounding music of an orchestra in rainy day

With tears rolling down like raindrops shining light blue
and the folded wings still gleaming in light
he was there just touching the soil
and I walked into his crying
only to be coming out as a flower

Cho Duk-haee
Board member of International PEN, Korea Center. Awarded Monthly Literature Space Prize.
Published poetry book *Secret Solitude* and more

꽃이 되어 나오더라

방금, 긴 터널을 벗어난
그의 숨소리는 울음이다
사계의 가장 낮은 음, 첫 도부터
열 옥타브쯤은 족히 견뎌 낸
추적추적 비 오는 날의
관현악기 울림이다.

희푸른 빗방울을 터트리며
이목구비마다 번뜩이는 날개를 접고
다만 착한 흙을 더듬는
그의 울음 속으로 내가 들어갔을 때
나는 꽃이 되어 나오더라.

조덕혜
국제펜한국본부 이사,
월간문학공간 본상 외,
시집 『비밀한 고독』
외.

The Mind of a Woman

Waiting for the spring
Mountains and meadows are clamoring

Red plume trees longing for lover
Shed red flowers like tears

Cherry blossoms are falling
In the spring cold snap

Along with awkward footsteps of a lover
The rustling sounds of the waving reeds
I hear coming from the windy forest

Jo Mi-ryeng
Poet, painter. Member of Korea Sinmunye Literature Association. Vice-president of Korea Arts Association. Published poetry book *The Color of Flowers*

여심

봄을 기다린 산과 들은
들썩들썩 요란한데

님 그리운 홍매화는
붉은 꽃 눈물 뿌리고

꽃샘추위에 벚꽃은
시린 꽃잎 떨구니

어색한 님의 발걸음
갈 숲 바람 소리만
사락사락 들린다

조미령
시인·화가, 한국신문예문
학회회원, 한국예술협회
부회장, 시집 『꽃빛』

Going Beyond the Walls between South and North Korea

A pigeon flies in between two walls
carrying a message of freedom and peace in its beak
flying towards the north with white wings fluttering

Although the wailing wall has been long gone
for the harmony of the east and the west, a wall kept in silence
still stands crying between South and North Korea

Ah, already it has been almost 80 years since the division
of the country by the DMZ built along the 3.8th parallel
making the distance between two walls felt so close and yet too far

Cho Young-mi
President of Women's Literature in Namyangju. Awarded Korean Women's Literature Prize. Published poetry book *Taking on a Train on Gyeonguchun Railway on a Snowy Day*

남과 북 장벽을 넘어서

벽과 벽 사이 비둘기 한 마리 날아든다
자유와 평화 메시지 한입 베어 물고
머언 북녘땅으로 흰 나래를 편다

이미 동서 화합으로 통곡의 벽
무너져내리고 남북 침묵의 벽은
세계를 향하여 소리 없는 아우성이다

아, 벌써 일흔두 살 지나 여든이 다
되어가는 비무장지대 DMZ 민통선 3.8선
너머
벽과 벽 사이는 너무도 가깝고 멀다

조영미
남양주여성문학회장, 한국여성문학상, 시집 『눈 내리는 날이면 경춘선을 탄다』

Mountains

Open your door locked in silence
I will hear the sad stories
That nobody hasn't informed yet

Baptized for forgiveness of sins they committed,
The clouds, birds, wild animals you played with,
They are running into the space known to nobody

Now, no more
Memories
Longings
The stories of long past
All get blown up

Totally stripped off the clothes
Failing to cover your shameful naked body,
I wonder, you were a sinner thrown away forever

Mountains
I ask you to open the door locked in silence

Cho Byung-moo
Poet, literary critic. Former professor at Dongduk Women's Uni. Awarded Green Literature Prize and more

산

너 침묵한 문을 열라
아무도 알려주지 않은
슬픈 이야기를 들으련다

천벌 한 몸에 세례받아
너와 함께 놀던 구름과 새와 짐승들은
어느 공간 속으로 달려가고 것이냐

이젠
추억도
동경도
먼 그날의 이야기도
일체 날려 버린 채

빠알갛게 벗겨진
너 부끄러운 나체를 가리지도 못하는
영원히 내쫓긴 죄인이였드냐

산아
너 침묵한 문을 열으렴

조병무
시인·문학평론가, 동덕
여대 문창과 교수 역임,
녹색문학상 수상 외.

People of Azaleas

If we go to the mountain, we can see the flower
If we go to the mountain, we can see the person
Mt. Baekdu, the mountain range connected by high ground
With the blossoms of azaleas spreading all over the mountains
the person is standing frozen in time like a longing statue
but also keeps herself too busy lighting a fire of flowers
Ah, the fire of flowers containing the soul of our people
Ah, the person living with azalea flowers blooming in our heart

If we go to the mountain, we can see the heart
If we go to the mountain, we can hear the song
Mt. Baekdu, the mountains and the streams are all connected
with the pure, white minds having a feast of flowers in the spring
The cheerful songs greeting the spring make us happy
lighting a fire of flowers in the heart regardless the season
Ah, the village we can enjoy Azalea flowers is our hometown
Ah, the songs we can hear at the place are songs of azaleas

Cho Hae
Member of International PEN, Korea Center & The Korean Writers Association. Board member of Korea Art Song Lyricists Association.

진달래 민족

그 산에 가면 그 산에 가면
그 꽃을 볼 수 있어요
그 산에 가면 그 산에 가면
그 사람 볼 수 있어요
백두산 백두산 끝없이 이어진 산맥
산에 산에 타 번지는 진달래 꽃불 속에
망부석으로 굳어져 있는 그 사람
치맛자락 날리며 꽃불을 지폈습니다
아, 그 꽃불 민족의 혼불입니다
아, 그 사람 진달래민족입니다

그 산에 가면 그 산에 가면 그 마을 볼 수
있어요
그 산에 가면 그 산에 가면 그 노래 들을
수 있어요
백두산 백두산 끝없이 이어진 산천
새봄이면 꽃잔치 흥겨운 새하얀 마을
귀맛 즐겁게 들려오는 꽃노래
계절 없이 가슴에 꽃불을 지펴줍니다
아, 그 마을 진달래 고향입니다
아, 그 노래 진달래 노래입니다

조 해
국제펜한국본부 회원,
한국문인협회 회원,
한국가곡작사가협회 이사

The Meaning of Love

Ah! How many long years
Have I struggled
To grasp the meaning of love?
How many words
Have I tried to fill with love?

Indeed,
Those who love do not seek
To understand the meaning of love.

Ah! Love is the gaze that sees you.
It is the heart that finds meaning
even in the single strand of your hair,
fine hairs beneath your ear
fluttering in the wind.

Chu Kwang-il
Member(PEN CLUB International, Korea), Attorney at law(Korea, DC USA), PhD in Law(Seoul National University)

사랑의 의미意味

아! 얼마나 오랜 세월을
나는 사랑의 의미를 캐기 위해서
고심했던가
얼마나 많은 언어에
사랑을 담으려고 했던가

그렇다
사랑하는 사람은 사랑의 의미를
알려 하지 않는다

아! 사랑은 당신을 보는 눈
당신의 머리카락 하나
바람에 날리는 당신의
귀밑털 하나에라도
의미를 부여하는 마음

주광일
국제PEN한국본부 회원, 변호사(한국, 미국 워싱턴 DC), 서울대 법학박사, 시집 『유형지로부터의 엽서』

A Fugue of the Ocean

The great power of the ocean
Pushing up the burning sun every morning

The power of the ocean coloring the ocean in blue
Giving rise to colorful rainbow over the waves
Opening the waterway, raising tunas, tooth shells,
Slightly deaf sturgeons as well
Making the isolated islands all connected with sea water

Without knowing the power of the ocean
We can neither cross it
Nor arrive at any of the island
Nor communicate each other

The great power of the ocean
Pushing up the burning sun every morning

With the power the ocean always stay as it is
With the power the ocean always stays the same
Without getting old

Ju Won-kyu
Advisory committee member of The Korean Writers Association. Awarded Korea Literature Centennial Prize. Published poetry book *The Face I Encountered by Chance*

바다 둔주곡遁走曲

매일 아침마다 햇덩이 하나씩
밀어 올리는 바다의 저 힘

그 힘이 바다를 푸르게 물들인다
파도 이랑마다 칠색 무지개를 띄운다
뱃길을 열고, 다랑어랑 뿔조개
가는귀먹은 철갑상어도 키운다
섬들을 엮어서 섬들을 섬이게 한다

바다의 저 힘을 모르고는
바다를 건널 수 없다
섬과 섬에 이를 수도 없고
네 말과 내 말을 섞을 수도 없다

매일 아침마다 햇덩이 하나씩
밀어 올리는 바다의 저 힘

그 힘으로 바다는 늘상 바다 곁에 있고
그 힘으로 바다는 항상
늙지 않는다

주원규
한국문인협회 자문위원, 한국문학100년상 외. 시집 『문득 만난 얼굴』 외.

About my Hometown

I don't know where my hometown is.
I think I heard it's in a mountain.
Or I remember it's on a sea.

Was I born as grass flower.
So I learned about roots in a mountain
And I learned about the sky on sea.

Every year
countless grass flowers bloom
and sing songs for peace.

Would you ask me again where my hometown is,
I'll answer it's Republic of Korea, or it's a global village.
Any places where flowers bloom to be my hometown.

Jee Eun-kyung
Poet, Ph. D in Literature & Literary critic. General president of Monthly Magazine Sinmunye. World Peace & Culture Prize and many more. Poems, Criticism, Columns and 30 other collections of essays.

내 고향은요

난, 고향이 어딘지 모릅니다
산이라 들은 것 같기도 하고
바다라 기억되기도 합니다

풀꽃으로 태어난 나는
산에서 뿌리를 배우고
바다에서 하늘을 배웠습니다

해마다 수많은 풀꽃들은
꽃을 피워내며
자유를 노래 부릅니다

고향이 어디냐고 또 물으신다면
내 고향은 대한민국이요 지구촌이요
꽃 피울 수 있는 곳은 모두 고향입니다

지은경
시인·문학평론가·문학
박사, 24·25대현대시
협 부이사장 역임, 세계
평화문화 대상 외. 시집
『사람아 사랑아』 외.

It's Time to Brush with Love

The heart waiting for the rainstorm
now calls for the butterflies by waving the flowers

It pushes the back of the butterflies
to fly down without wavering
between longing and waiting

Who knows the mind of the wind, I wonder,
asking for the butterflies to come down
on the smudge of the melting snow

It's a secret nobody knows but you
that you have been here before anybody

Finally love fills the lightened body of flowers
awaking the time of longing

Getting one step closer to each other
the wind makes the flowers bloom in full
brushing the whole world in blue

Chae Ja-kyung
Member of International PEN, Korea Center. Awarded Korean Writers Prize and more.
Published poetry book *A Ladder of Magnolia*

사랑을 칠할 시간

비바람을 기다리던 마음이
꽃 흔들어 나비를 부릅니다

그리움과 기다림 사이에
머뭇거리던 나비가 앉을까, 말까
망설임에 등 떠밀어 봅니다

녹는 눈이 남긴 얼룩자국 위로
바람결이 나비를 부르기 전
바람의 마음을 누가 알까

그대가 먼저 다녀갔다는 것은
너도 모르고, 나도 모르는 비밀

사랑이 드디어 가벼워진 꽃의 몸
갈망의 시간을 깨운다

한 발자국씩 서로는 다가서서
씨앗 피울 온 천지
파릇한 붓질이다

채자경
국제펜한국본부 회원,
한국문학인상 외, 시집
『목련꽃 사다리』

The Words of Reeds

Reeds catch the light wind with silky hair tufts
Yes, they do
They use the heads for the words sounding good

Reeds catch the gentle breeze with the stems
Yes, they do
They want to hear better the words in low voice

Reeds withstand the moderate wind with the strong roots
Yes, they do
They endure the harsh words with patience

Reeds let the stiff wind go through the leaves
Yes, they do
They let loud noises go in one ear and out the other

To sum up,
Putting all sorts of words together
Those words are just like the winds blowing through the reeds

---

Choi Kye-sik
Made literary debut through *Poetry & Poetics* in 1961. Guidance committee member of Korea Modern Poets Association. Published poetry book *Travel of Flowers*

갈대의 말씀

솔솔이 바람은 잔털 꽃대로 맞아요
그럼은요
듣기 좋은 말은 반드시 머리로요

여린 바람일수록 온통 줄기로 받아요
그래요
낮은 소리니까 더 크게 들어야지요

헤살이 바람결은 밑둥으로 견디구요
그럼은요
싫은 말일수록 눌러서 삭히세요

센 바람은요 잎 사이로 빗겨 버려요
그래요
큰소리는 그냥 한 귀로 흘리셔야죠

그러니까
이런저런 말들 다 놓아 보면은
벼라별 소리 모두 갈대 바람이네요

최계식
1961년 시전문지
≪시와 시론≫ 등단,
한국현대시인협회 지도
위원, 시집『꽃들의 여행』외.

The Ocean in Spring

The ocean in spring strokes my forehead
with hands as soft as mother's breast

Over the sandy shore are scattered memories of hometown, of the time I was young, dreaming about my future

The seeds of endless curiosity and passion for adventure sometimes have grown to be huge waves putting me at risk

Nevertheless, they always gave me the strength
and the energy to keep going on the journey for my dream

Now, despite me feeling like a stone statue of grandmother with the body getting old and weak in the stiff wind

Always greeting me with the warm affection of mother's arms the ocean in spring stands at the corner of my old hometown

---

Choi Young-hee
Poet, singer of classic songs. President of essay division in Asian Pacific Writers Association. Awarded the 20th Whang Jin-hee Literature Prize. Member of Classic Song Lovers Association in Daegu

봄 바다

봄 바다가 어머니의 젖가슴처럼
부드러운 손길로 이마를 쓸어주네

모래사장 한가득 부린 고향의 추억
어릴 적, 너를 보며 이상을 꿈꾸었네

끝없는 호기심과 모험의 씨앗들은 자라
큰 파도가 되어 휘몰아치곤 했지만

인생의 여정을 항해하는 나에게
항상 힘을 주던 내 꿈의 터전이었네

이제 서서히 삭아져 내리는 육신
세찬 바람 맞으며 돌할망 되어도

내 고향 봄 바다는 어머니 품처럼
집으로 돌아가는 정겨운 길목 같네

최영희
시인·성악가, 아태문협
수필분과위원장, 제20
회 황진이문학상, 현)
대구가곡사랑회원.

Blooming Flowers

Shivering in the cold
the leaves yet embrace flower buds softly
putting them together strand by strand in green
weaving them into yellow chrysanthemum petals one by one
The leaves hanging down in the cold
being held in the arms of light green
rub their cheeks as if caressing each other

From a dewdrop rolling around
on the leaves propping tender petals in green
carrying the soft sunlight imbued with fragrance of autumn
I see the bright eyes of flowers clean and innocent
reading the modest and quiet mind on the bright yellow petals
embracing each other with the arms wide spread

Choi Ihn-seok
Made literary debut through *Sisun* in 2011. Retired from Agency for Defense Development. Published poetry book *Wavelength of Sounds*

꽃을 피우다

시린 이파리 사르르 떨며
보시시 꽃망울 안고 있다
초록빛 한 올 한 올 이어서
한 잎 한 잎 노란 국화 꽃잎 엮고 있다
한기에 숙인 잎사귀마저
연둣빛으로 감싸 안으며
애무하듯 볼을 비빈다

여린 꽃잎 푸르게 받치며
가을 향 배어든 볕살을 싣는다
또르르 구르는 이슬 한 방울에서
무구無垢한 꽃송이의 영롱한 눈망울을 본다
샛노란 꽃잎에 함초롬 젖은 마음
서로는 두 팔 벌려 안고 있다

최인석
2011년 《시선》으로 등단, 국방과학연구소 퇴임, 시집 『소리의 파장』

The Sound of Opening the Dawn

Tap, taptap, the sound of raindrops knocking on the window
Rain splattering against street pavement
Those raindrops reminds me of the ones I heard
walking on the gravels at the back yard of the old house
considering the raindrops opening a day
of the past a very long time ago
When the rain stopped, I felt like I heard even the quietude,
the sounds of the wind passing through the woven fence
Raindrops at the tip of persimmon leaves fell
making noise of falling rain all of a sudden
waking up the tree branches to do stretching out
Again I felt like I heard the sounds of grass leaves rustling
and of the world awaking in the quietude after the rain
The sound of opening the universe and opening the dawn
The sounds of footsteps my father made going to work

Choi Choon
Member of The Korean Writers Association. Awarded Sunbway Poetry Contest Prize. Published a book *As if the Moon Shines on a thousand Rivers*

새벽을 여는 소리

톡 토도독 창 두드리는 빗소리
자박자박 시멘트 바닥 걷는 빗소리
그리움 불러오는 정겨운 빗소리는
오랜 세월 저편
고향 집 뒤뜰 자갈밭을 내디디며
새벽을 여는 소리 같다
그 소리 멈추면 고요까지 들렸다
울타리 사이 지나가는 바람 소리
감나무 이파리 끝 빗방울이
한꺼번에 후드득 떨어질 만큼
나뭇가지 기지개 켜는 소리
빗물에 낮추었다 일어서는 풀잎 소리
세상이 깨어나는 고요까지 들렸다
우주를 열고 새벽을 여는 소리,
일터로 향하는 아버지 발자국 소리

최 춘
한국문인협회 회원, 지하철 시 공모 당선, 저서 『하나의 달이 천 개의 강을 비추듯』

A Lunar Halo

Right before bursting out crying
her eyeballs still retained sorrow deeply suppressed

Her eyes were swelling up
as if she would sob her heart out any time
upon a slight touch

With her first child buried in her heart
the eyes of my sister were up in the sky
being suspended, having a lunar halo

Ha Gab-soo
Former principal at elementary school, former school commissioner at the Office of Education in Kyungnam Province. Awarded Commendation from the minister of education. Published poetry book, *The Road Took Belatedly*

달무리

울음 토하기 전
슬픔을 억누르고 있는 눈망울

사알짝 건들면
금방이라도 눈물 쏟을 것 같은
부푼 눈동자

첫 자식 떠나보낸
누이의 눈이
하늘에 걸렸네

하갑수
전 경상남도 교육청 장학사, 전 초등학교 교장, 교육부장관 표창,
시집 『뒤늦은 길』

The Ocean As It Alway Has Been

I always miss the ocean waves with heavy heart
for they splash on the old heart of mine

The sea breeze makes me feel heart-rending pain
for it makes me take out old faded pictures one by one

Seagulls always make my eyes wet
for they help me untie the package of sad stories off the mind

The horizon of the sea always gets in my mind with pain
for it embraces the cowardly timid soul of mine with sympathy

I like to load my flesh and soul onto a ship leaving the port
for the ship makes a nostalgic gesture with the sun-washed flag

Always aspiring to see the person like crazy
I want to become the ocean, finally to be with the person

Han Ki-hong
Poet, essayist. President of International PEN, Korea Center, Inchon Branch. Published poetry book *The Autumn Sky in Van Gogh's Canvas*

늘 바다인 것을

파도가 늘 먹먹하게 그리운 것은
철썩철썩 묵은 가슴 두드리기 때문인 것을

해풍이 늘 아프게 시려오는 것은
빛바랜 옛 사진 하나씩 시나브로
끄집어내기 때문인 것을

갈매기가 늘 눈시울을 적시게 하는 것은
끼룩끼룩 꺼이꺼이 설움 봇짐 풀어주기
때문인 것을

수평선이 늘 왼 가슴 아리게 담겨오는 것은
가녀린 새가슴 애처로운 심혼을 보듬기
때문인 것을

저 어선 한 척에 늘 영육을 적재하고
싶은 것은
오라, 떠나자 부르는 표백 된 노스탈쟈
손짓 때문인 것을

그래서 그 사람이 늘 미치도록 보고파지는
것은 바다가 되어 마침내 하나가 되고 싶기
때문인 것을

한기홍
시인·수필가, 국제펜한
국본부 인천지역 회장.
시집 『가을하늘 고흐의
캔버스』 외.

Sitting in Front of a Tea Cup

Regretting of not having repeated one more time
under the lamp shedding light exposing the bare skin
listening to the sad stories of someone
I fell in the oblivion wavering for a while
and tried to go towards the dim light I first encountered
I was struggling to figure out the distinction
between happiness and unhappiness which gets vague
With unshackled chain of desire hidden in the hard time
I have endured standing on tiptoes
I smashed the empty space in vain
But the anxiety I felt holding me tight
still takes a place in my empty head
building a nest that would be kept in secret forever

Han Seong-geun
Born in Bosung, Jeonnam. Awarded The Better Literature Prize. Published poetry book *Time that Cannot be Filled*

찻잔을 앞에 두고

한 번도 되뇌어 보지 못한 아쉬움에 휘둘리어
희부연 속살 내비친 가로등 아래서
누군가의 서러운 이야기 들을 적이면
망각의 너울 속에 잠시 들러
처음 마주한 미명을 향해 어디로든 가보려고
일찌감치 바동거려보다가
행복과 불행의 구분이 모호해져
까치발 딛고 서서 견디어 낸 힘겨운 시간만큼
숨어 있던 욕망의 사슬을 풀어헤쳐
애먼 허공이라도 후려쳐보자는
마음 조인 안타까운 생각이 사라질 듯 말 듯
영원히 새 나가지 않을 비밀처럼
텅 빈 머릿속에 둥우리를 틀고 있었다

한성근
전남 보성 출생, 더좋은
문학상 수상, 시집 『채
워지지 않는 시간』 외.

Large Snowflakes

In moonlight shining as bright
as a silky fortune pocket in orange color
the snow was falling in the middle of a night
Being afraid of posing any burden
to the dreamers' dream
the snow was falling, fluttering in the air
Like flowers in limpid eyes of spotted deers
soothing pains of the world
keeping the dreamers warm in large snowflakes

Hur Man-gil
Ph.D. in Literature. Poet. Novelist. Founder of Complex Literature (1971). Board Member of PEN International, Korea Center. Awards: 'The Pure Literature Award for Writers', etc. Collection of Poems: 'In History and in Life', etc.

함박눈

연주황 빛 복주머니 웃음 같은
달이 만든 그 빛줄 따라
한밤에 눈이 내렸다.
꿈꾸는 사람들의
꿈이 무거울까 봐
하늘거리는 가벼움으로 내렸다.
꽃사슴 눈빛처럼 착한 꽃잎으로
세상 아픔 다 잠재우며
꿈이 포근한 쌓인 함박눈

허만길
문학박사·시인·소설가,
복합문학(Complex
Literture) 창시(1971).

Snail

To write a poem titled "Snail"
I wrote "Snail"
but read it "Staying home all the time"

COVID-19 makes people carry
a house on the back like a snail

Heo Hyung-man
Poet, literary critic. Honorary professor at Mokpo Univ. Published poetry book, *Grass Blade's Prayer To the Lord* and more

달팽이

'달팽이'라는 제목으로 시를 쓰기 위해
'달팽이'라고 써놓고
읽기는 '집콕'으로 읽는다

코로나는 사람을 모두
달팽이처럼 집을 짊어지게 했다.

허형만
시인·평론가, 목포대학교 명예교수, 시집 『풀잎이 하나님에게』 외.

Pretty Pebbles

Pretty smooth pebbles lying all over the seashore
have suffered from the waves, the winds, people's trampling
along with other pebbles sliding across each other

On a journey of a life running towards our dreams
we meet people, greeting, understanding each other
holding hands together, expressing gratitude, cultivating a better life

Living a life overcoming the intangible winds, waves, and trampling
makes the traces of our life left on the face
May you become a beautiful pebble being loved by everyone

Hong Kyung-ja
Member of The Korean Writers Association. Awarded The 37th PEN Literature Prize. Published poetry book *Does Resonance Exist in My Life?* and more

예쁜 조약돌이

해변 자갈밭에 널린 예쁘고 매끈한 조약돌
오랜 세월 파도와 바람과 사람들의 발굽에 시달리고
크고 작은 돌들과 부대끼며 씨름도 하였다

꿈을 향하여 달려가는 인생길
맺어진 인연에 서로의 눈을 맞추고 마음을 헤아리며
손에 손을 맞잡고 감사하며 삶의 텃밭을 가꾸어간다

만져지지 않는 바람과 파도와 발굽을 이겨내는 일생
얼굴에 삶의 흔적이 남는다
모든 이에게 사랑받는 예쁜 조약돌이 되기를…

홍경자
한국문협회원, 제37회 PEN문학상 외, 시집 『내 삶에는 울림이 있는가』 외.

Gwanghwamun Square is Becoming a Hot Place

Despite freezing temperature below zero in Celsius,
so many people are gathering at Gwanghwamun Square

Brachio figurine tube characters are waving themselves
to make the world more beautiful

Shops around the Square are closed for the cold
but still we can enjoy ourselves at the Lantern Festival

Maidens of light are standing at the center of the Square
with pretty and elegant postures

Making a great photo zone so attractive
for the crowds gathering around to take pictures

People are standing in lines to see all kinds of attractions
in the form of colorful lanterns

Hackberry trees near the entrance of the Square play a role
for the festival offering the shade

Hong In-sook
Poet, coffee barista. Member of The Korean Writers Association. Awarded Citation from the head of Nowongu district office, Published poetry book *Condor, Condor*

광화문 광장은 뜨고 있네요

광화문 광장의 인파는 영하의 날씨에도
엄청나구요

브라키오는 아름다운 세상을 만들겠다고
파도를 이네요

추위에 상점은 자물통을 굳게 채워도
틈새로 눈요기해요

광장의 중앙엔 빛의 처녀가 곱게
품격을 갖추어

포토존을 만들고 관객의 발끝을
유혹해 법석이죠

발걸음 늦추게 볼거리로 행인 줄은
늘어만 가고

광장 입구엔 차오르는 팽나무가 정자나무로
한몫 하지요

홍인숙
시인·커피바리스타,
한국문인협회 회원,
노원구청장 표창장,
시집 『콘도르 콘도르』

Autumn

Cold wind rising from afar
brings winter to the garden now
where my heart lies down with fallen leaves

Like the children trying to collect
the stories of the birds and the flowers
the hands of autumn is so clumsy

Being knotted together with the death
autumn stands firm in the field after harvest
only as a scarecrow

Autumn
like the clumsy hands of children
always appears sad

Hong Jung-gi
War correspondent for Vietnam's Nha Trang and Saigon Broadcasting Inc. Chairman of The Korean War Literature. Published poetry book, *Baby Steps*

가을

먼-뎬 차가운 바람 일어
겨울을 몰고 오고 지금 뜨락엔
모인 마음이 눕는다

새들과 꽃들의 이야기를 모으려는
마음처럼이나 가을은 철부지 아이들의
손놀림

가을은 죽음으로 매어나
추수 끝난 벌판에 허수아비로만
우뚝 서다

가을은
철부지 아이들의 손놀림처럼이나
슬픈 것

홍중기
한국전쟁문학회 회장,
베트남 나트랑·사이공
방송국 근무(종군기자),
시집 『아기 걸음마』

The Time I Spent with My Love

On a cheerful day with bright sunshine
using lye as a detergent
I washed ramie clothes clean
and hung them out on a clothesline
feeling so refreshed
even at the tip of my fingers

The time I spent with my love made me feel
as refreshed as I washed ramie clothes clean

Hwang Sun-ho
Poet, essayist, freelancer photographer. Made literary debut through *Modern Poetry Literature*

내 여자와의 시간

햇빛 쾌활한 날
잿물에
때 쏙 뺀 하얀 모시옷을
깍듯이 널고 나면
손끝에서부터 오는
아, 이 개운한 맛!

내 여자와의 시간은
하얀 모시 빨래 같은 개운함이었다.

황선호
시인·수필가, 프리랜서
사진작가, 현대시문학
등단.

Everything's Fine

Drinking a tea of bitter gourd
I ask myself
what I live for

With my mobile phone at repose during the weekend
expecting no visitors to come, I still strain my ears
for the door bell to ring by any chance

With the sunset glowing red
in the color of azalea flowers
being alone without whom I enjoyed his companionship
I find myself missing him so much today

Sitting on a chair
looking at the clouds flying in the sky
I feel, though, the wings for infinite freedom grow on me

Being left alone made me feel
such a deep loneliness and sorrow;
now for me as a person of free will, everything's fine

Hwang Ok-rye
Poet, essayist. The 8th president of Korea Sinmunye Literature Association. Awarded Hwang Jin-hee Literature Prize. Published poetry book *Eyes of Wooden Fish* and more

괜찮아, 괜찮아

무엇을 위해 살고 있는지
씁쓸한 여주 차를 마시며
내가 나에게 묻는다

주말, 핸드폰 벨은 휴식 중
찾아온다 약속한 사람 없어도
현관 벨 소리 울리나 귀 기울인다

붉게 물든 저녁노을은
영산홍꽃 빛깔로 고운데
함께 즐기던 사람 떠나고 없으니
오늘 그 사람 더욱 그리워진다

의자에 앉아
하늘을 날고 있는 구름 떼를 보며
무한한 자유의 날개 돋아난다

홀로 남는다는 건
지독한 외로움이요 슬픔이지만
자유인이여, 괜찮아 괜찮아.

황옥례
시인·수필가, 한국신문
예문학회 제8대 회장,
황진이문학상 대상,
시집 『목어의 눈』 외.

Dokdo Island

For the country of the morning sun rising
the Dokdo island has been resisting the heavy waves
with the spirit of Mt. Baekdu made by the sunlight
to protect the roots of the peninsular

The rocky island standing upright with mountain peaks
having the flaring souls of five thousand years of history
The Dokdo island represents the soul of Koreans

Once the Japanese government occupied the country by force
but now listen to the breathing sounds of ocean waves
Nobody can deny the island is ours or steal it from us by any means

With all of us singing to make it clear that "Dokdo island is ours"
Dokdo island protecting our country would never be left alone lonely

---

Hwang Ju-cheol
Board member of Albatross Poetry Reciting Association. Member of International PEN, Korea Center & The Korean Writers Association.

독도

해 뜨는 아침의 나라
백두의 숨결 햇살로 빚어
높은 파도 이겨내며
한반도 뿌리를 지켜왔다

우뚝 서 있는 돌섬
봉우리마다 반만년 역사의 혼불
독도는 한국인의 영혼이다

한때 일본의 침략이 있었지만
끓어오르는 바다의 숨소리 들어보라
훔칠 수도 삼킬 수도 없는 대한의 땅이다

오늘도 "독도는 우리땅" 노래 부르며
조국을 지키는 독도는 외롭지 않다

황주철
알바트로스시낭송문협
이사, 국제펜한국본부
회원, 한국문협 회원.

K-POETRY
Getting on the Wings of Peace
한국시 평화의 날개 달다

Copyright 2024
All rights reserved by The Korean Writers Association
No part of this book may be reproduced in any form without written permission of the copyright owner, except for the use of brief quotation in a book review.

Published by Cheaknara Publishing Co.
14 Nokbon-ro 3 Gagil, Eunpyung-gu,
Seoul, Republic of Korea 03377

Phone +82-02-389-0146
Fax   +82-02-389-0147
E-mail sinmunye@hanmail.net
http   cafe.daum.net/sinmunye
Price $ 30

이사장 김호운
펴낸이 지은경
번 역 김인영
펴낸곳 도서출판 책나라

초판 1쇄 발행 / 2024년 9월 30일

㈜03377 서울시 은평구 녹번로 3가길 14, 라임하우스 1층 101호
(02)389-0146~7, (02)289-0147
E-mail / sinmunye@hanmail.net
http://cafe.daum.net/sinmunye
등록번호 제110-91-10104호(2004.1.14)

ⓒ 지은경, 2024
ISBN 979-11-92271-33-0

값 40,000원